ESSAYS ON EVALUATION OF THE EFFECTIVENESS OF PUBLIC HEALTH
PROGRAMS ON CHILD'S WELL-BEING: EVIDENCE FROM INDONESIA
FAMILY LIFE SURVEY

By

Elan Satriawan

A DISSERTATION

Submitted to
Michigan State University
in partial fulfillment of the requirement
for the degree of

DOCTOR OF PHILOSOPHY

Agricultural Economics

2009

UMI Number: 3364743

INFORMATION TO USERS

The quality of this reproduction is dependent upon the quality of the copy
submitted. Broken or indistinct print, colored or poor quality illustrations and
photographs, print bleed-through, substandard margins, and improper
alignment can adversely affect reproduction.

In the unlikely event that the author did not send a complete manuscript
and there are missing pages, these will be noted. Also, if unauthorized
copyright material had to be removed, a note will indicate the deletion.

ABSTRACT

ESSAYS ON EVALUATION OF THE EFFECTIVENESS OF PUBLIC HEALTH PROGRAMS ON CHILD'S WELL-BEING: EVIDENCE FROM INDONESIA FAMILY LIFE SURVEY

By

Elan Satriawan

This dissertation consists to two essays. The first essay evaluates the impact of childhood nutritional status and the presence of a public health program on subsequent child schooling in Indonesia during 1990s. We estimate dynamic relationship of childhood nutrition and subsequent child schooling in which we carefully address the potential correlation between childhood nutrition and important but unobserved factors such as child innate healthiness and parents' taste toward child quality. We find that reducing incidence of poor childhood nutrition reduces also the probability of delayed enrollment, but not the probability of repeating a grade. More importantly, the estimated effects when taking into account the endogeneity of childhood nutrition are 5-7 times stronger than when ignoring the endogeneity of childhood nutrition.

The effect of childhood nutrition on subsequent child schooling is even higher if child has access to public health facilities. Looking particularly at presence of midwife, we find that the presence of midwife magnifying the effect of childhood nutritional status on subsequent child schooling. This result suggests that the exposure to midwife during early childhood improved child nutritional status that in turn helped child schooling.

The second essay evaluates the effectiveness of a supplementary feeding program for maintaining child nutritional status through the period of the 1997-1998 economic crises in Indonesia. We exploit heterogeneity in program exposure to evaluate the program effect. The use of program heterogeneity has at least two advantages for identifying the effect of Indonesia's supplemental feeding program. First use of program exposure allows us to estimate an effect even with low variation of program distribution across targeted subjects. Second, use of the program allows us to avoid the strong assumption that all targeted children experienced homogenous exposure to the program.

We show that although the program tended to be universally distributed during 1998-2000, the distribution of program length varied across communities. We also provide insight into the government's implicit allocation rule when determining program length. Findings on the effect of program exposure show that the program improved the nutritional status of children 12 to 23 months of age during the period of economic crisis. Our findings also suggest that the program helped children with severe malnutrition problems.

Our results also highlight the potential benefit of using heterogeneity in program exposure when evaluating a universally targeted program. The use of program intensity is not just helpful to capture program effects as it can also be used to in conjunction with community fixed effects in a way that avoids bias from endogenous program placement.

ACKNOWLEDGEMENTS

Al ḥamdu lillāhi rabbi l-'ālamīn, All praise is to Allah, the Lord of the universe, for all of His blessings that makes all of these things happen and allows me to complete this dissertation.

I would like to express my sincere gratitude to all persons that help to make the completion of this task possible. First, I am deeply indebted to Professor John Giles, my dissertation supervisor for all his guidance and very kind support during the writing process of the dissertation. I have been greatly fortunate to have him as advisor that treats me more as a colleague rather than just student supervisee. I would also thank to my major Professor Richard Bernsten for his support and guidance I have received since I joined the program in 2003 until now. I also owe my gratitude to my external committee member, Professor John Strauss of University of Southern California who always provides me with promptly advises when I ask him. He has set a high standard for his students and his sharp and critical advises have contributed a lot in shaping my dissertation and the way I think about empirical work as it is now. I also want to thank to my other committee members Professor Eric Crawford and John Staatz for their support and guidance during my study time and dissertation writing process.

I am also indebted to some of friends and colleagues with whom I intellectually discussed and debated many issues in the development areas. Particularly I would like to thank to Firman Witolear, (late) Lesiba Bopape, Lilian Kirimi, Denis Nizalov, Shauffique Shidique, Merry Matenge, Anthony Chapoto, Elliot Mehgenye, Abdoul Kareem Murekezi, Kirimi Sindi, Vandana Yadav, Athur Mabiso, and Sarma Aralas.

I want to also thank to Indonesian and Malaysian community for their warm reception during our stay in East Lansing, particularly to Firman Witoelar & Nina, Mas Diwan & Mbak Susi, Pak and Bu Ronnie, Haryono and Ria, Dwi Agus, Reza and Nana, Shaufique and Nita, Azril and Bismi and other community members that I can not mention one by one here.

Special thank also goes to member of Indonesia Islamic Study Group: Mas Eka, Mas Ahmad, Mas Endra, Mas Danet, Kang Dena, Bang Torkis, Ristanto, Didi and their respective family. They have become my family during my stay in US and with them I manage to maintain my insanity and to deal with stress I obtained from life as student.

Now it is turn to express my gratitude to my family back home. I deeply believe that of the main ingredients of this achievement are unconditional love and blessing from my parents and parents in-law. To my parents, Ibu and Bapak, and my parents in-law Ibu and (late) Bapak Ronnie, I would never be able to pay back all of those that you have given to me. Only Allah will grant you with much better ones in this world and afterlife. Also to my brother, sister and sister in-law and their family–Mas Ari & Mbak Miska, Mbak Esti & Mas Iprin, and Mb Ria & Mas Mirza— sincere love and attentions you dedicate to me can lift-up my spirit and motivation to get the job done as soon as I can.

Most importantly, none of this would have been possible without the role of my wife and my children. My wife, Rennta Chrisdiana (Awie) has been someone who is always there for me, provided me with the genuine love, bottomless patience and unconditional support. My children, Lila, Haikal, Raisa and Khalif, they have become a place where I can melt all depressed and frustrated feelings, made my days become bright again after thousands time of feeling down. I should say that completing this study and getting the degree is not only my personal achievement. It is theirs too. It is my and their achievement.

TABLE OF CONTENT

LIST OF TABLES

LIST OF FIGURES

CHAPTER 1

INTRODUCTION

Governments in developing countries are spending increasing sums of money to invest in human resources and in improving the quality of life of their populations. Like public investments for infrastructure like the building roads and bridges, schools, and hospitals, public investment in human resources are now also supported through a rationale of providing public goods. Increasing investment in human development is reflected in devotion of resources to recruit teachers, medical doctors, midwifes, nurses as well as creating curriculum, providing medicine to public health providers, and funding supplementary feeding programs.

One irony in the use of such public resources is that governments neither know whether these investments any effect on the welfare of the targeted people as intended, nor what the magnitudes of these effects might be. The situation becomes worse as the governments of developing countries often scale up the public program without the sufficient and credible knowledge of program effectiveness. We might argue that there would be a portion of the investment that would benefit the poor and the needy. Without sufficient knowledge on how the program might affect the people, this portion might be minimal and thus the investment may not be socially efficient.

Designing and implementing a credible program evaluation is always not an easy task. Other than the approaches that that have been developed recently, they require data that are not widely available, including multiple cross-section data, panel data, and data from randomized experiments. Therefore the absence of credible impact evaluation for public programs in developing countries reflects not only the absence of the skill to design and execute, but also the scarcity of the resources.

Appropriate data are becoming more available, particularly survey data, and some new evaluation methods are readily used now. Survey data are not specifically designed for the purpose of conducting impact evaluation, but rapid development of methods to implement impact evaluation has been empowering researchers to utilize it.[1] An alternative approach which is becoming common involves use of randomized experiments. The approach has some advantageous over the ones that use survey data particularly in dealing with selection bias. However it also has some disadvantages: first, randomized evaluations require a lot of resources if implemented in a large scale, and second, they often face ethical issues when it the experiments relate with interventions to the poor.[2] The two essays on impact evaluation in this dissertation use survey data and focus on evaluating policy interventions designed to improve the health and nutritional status of children.

---

[1] See Ravallion (2007) for detail review on various methods of impact evaluation.
[2] See Duflo et al (2007) for motivation, toolkits and reviews of randomized experiments.

The importance of nutritional status and its economic implications have been well-documented in the development literature. For the early age groups, better nutrition for children is associated with lower risk in child mortality and morbidity. Better nutrition at young ages also explains, in part, higher productivity during later stages of growth. Studies have also found the association between adult health and earnings [see for example Martolell and Arroyave (1988), Behrman and Deolalikar (1988), Behrman (1996), and Strauss and Thomas (1998)].

With a focus on developing economies, much of the attention in this literature have been focused on the relation between the weather-related and other shocks with the health and nutritional outcomes of individuals. Many papers also have been written in this literature on how households might respond to the shocks and on the effectiveness of the adopted shock-coping mechanisms. A main result from these studies show that not all households, particularly those that face liquidity constraints, can smooth consumption and thus can maintain their health and nutritional status (see the survey in Dercon, 1993).

Nevertheless some important questions have received little attention in this literature. For instance, while the current literature mainly focused on short-run and transitory effect of the shocks, the question of whether and how shocks may have long-run and permanent effects is relatively unanswered. In addition, inadequate attention has been made to answer how heterogeneity in public

3

program 'intensity' (which may include quality, duration or exposure) affects the impact on individuals' health.[3] In addition, researchers and policy analysts have only recently paid attention to the longer-run relationship between early childhood nutrition with child other human capital aspects such as subsequent academic achievement. There remains much to be done in these areas.

Our purpose here is to address such unanswered issues to complement current literature. We divide this study into two essays. The first one, in chapter 2, examines the impact of preschool-age child nutritional status on child's subsequent academic attainment. In addition, taking into account the availability and the quality of local health programs, the essay will evaluate the effect of government health policy on academic attainment. Evidence of the positive impact of early childhood nutrition on educational achievement would document the importance of nutritional investment during childhood and provide a justification for government intervention such as supplementary feeding program. In addition, the evidence on the impact of public health programs, if any, on health status of children during early age would provide support for government policies providing this type of public investment.

The next essay, in chapter 3, evaluates the impact of a supplementary food program for preschool age children in Indonesia on child nutritional status by making use of heterogeneity in the duration of program exposure. The analysis

---

[3] King and Behrman (2008) discuss the use of timing and duration of exposure on evaluation of social programs and how it might generate different impacts than measurement with simple binary program exposure.

makes use of heterogeneity program duration to evaluate the impact on child's nutritional status and thus makes an important contribution to the program evaluation literature.

This study uses data from all publicly available waves of Indonesia Family Life Survey (IFLS) up to now: 1993, 1997 and 2000. The first (1993) and second (1997) wave of the surveys were carried out by RAND Corp of Santa Monica and Demographic Institute. While the third (2000) wave was conducted by RAND Corp and Center for Population and Policy Studies, Gadjah Mada University. IFLS is panel/longitudinal data that collects rich information on the socio-economic characteristics of individuals, households and communities where they resided as well as public facilities they utilized. This brings us one advantage to link household and community-facilities surveys enabling us to establish connection between the outcomes or impact we expect to see at the individual level with the policy change that is observed as changes in community and facilities where these individuals lived.

Our general findings from first essay show that childhood nutritional status was important for subsequent schooling outcomes, and differed in impact for boys and girls. The results also imply that previous studies that do not taking into account potential source of bias suffer underestimate the effect. In addition, we find that presence of a village midwife in the community in fact magnifies the positive effect of childhood nutrition on child schooling implying that a village midwife complements nutritional status in early childhood.

5

Findings from second essay indicate that a supplemental feeding program was effective but that its impact was limited only to infants under 24 months. Children from older age groups were not affected by the program. We also find that the exposure to the program reduced the likelihood of stunting within the same age group.

CHAPTER 2

EVALUATING THE IMPACT OF EARLY CHILDHOOD NUTRITION AND AVAILABILITY OF HEALTH SERVICE PROVIDERS ON SUBSEQUENT CHILD SCHOOLING: EVIDENCE FROM INDONESIA FAMILY LIFE SURVEY

2.1. Introduction

Due to the perceived importance of both health status and education of children for both current well-being and their future productivity as adults, much attention in both the research and policy communities has focused on early childhood nutritional status and the enrollment of children in school. With strong interest in these areas, studies documenting correlations between these dimensions of child human capital and subsequent well-being as adults have multiplied in recent years.[4] In addition, empirical research has also attempted to identify intermediate factors affecting the relationship between child health schooling, and thus also affecting the outcomes of children as adults. The general assumption about the direction of influence between child health and educational investments is that child outcomes in school are more favorable with improvements in early childhood nutrition.

While the findings from a substantial body of existing research suggest that child nutrition is important for child schooling outcomes, many of these studies suffer from serious bias and fail to establish a causal relationship between

---

[4] For most recent review in related studies see Glewwe and Miguel (2007) and Strauss and Thomas (2007).

child nutritional status and child schooling.[5] The most important source of bias stems from a failure to take into account the fact that both child schooling and child health status reflect household decisions. Many studies estimate the effect of early childhood nutrition on subsequent child schooling outcomes assuming that there is no correlation between childhood nutrition and important unobserved factors such as child innate ability, parent preferences toward child quality, or parent gender preferences.

Although estimation controlling for this source of endogeneity may still be sensitive to underlying household behavioral assumptions and the nature of unobserved heterogeneity, research by Behrman and Lavy (1998), has shown that estimates of the effect of childhood nutrition on child schooling are biased downward when early childhood nutrition is treated as exogenous. Behrman and Lavy (1998) further demonstrate that if estimation assumes that (i) child health is correlated with unobserved individual, household and community level heterogeneity such as genetic endowment, home study environment, or availability of education facilities, and (ii) that if there are no unobserved inputs into child cognitive development and prices can be used as instruments, then the impact of health status on educational outcomes is three to seven times as large as those when ignoring endogeneity of child health. The bias is even larger when the second assumption is dropped.

---

[5]See the reviews in Pollit (1990), Behrman (1996) and Behrman and Lavy (1998).

Studies using only cross-section data frequently suffer from an additional source of bias. Typically they estimate current period child nutritional status on contemporaneous child schooling or use recall methods to measure past childhood nutrition and estimate an effect on current period child schooling. While it is difficult to argue that the parameters estimated from the former approach can be used to establish a causal relationship between health and schooling outcomes within the same period, parameters estimated using retrospective information are likely to suffer from recall bias. Once we recognize these concerns, it is difficult to imagine that causality between childhood nutrition and child schooling can be established using cross-sectional survey data.

To date there are four significant studies exploiting panel data which examine the relationship between nutritional status and child schooling and also address the methodological concerns noted above.[6] Alderman et al (2001), use panel data from rural Pakistan and find that child nutritional status affected school enrollment, and that the impact was greater for girls than for boys. Their preferred estimate employs a dynamic model and uses price shocks at the time when children were of 5 years old as instrumental variables.[7] Their results show

---

[6]See Alderman, Behrman, Lavy and Menon (2001); Alderman, Hoddinott, and Kinsey (2006); Glewwe, Jacoby and King (2001), and Ghuman, Behrman, Gultiano and King (2006).
[7]The choice of price shocks as instruments avoids the strong identifying assumption that there is no correlation between child height-for-age up to age two and after two years of age, as in Glewwe et al (2001). Still, one might be concerned about the timing of the price shocks used. As they also note, price shocks at age 5 might not adequately capture health status of children when of preschool age. Strauss and Thomas (2007) also note the potential for long-term effects of shocks

that when one controls for endogeneity in child nutritional status, its effect was three times more important for enrollment than when the model was estimated without controlling for endogeneity in childhood nutrition.

Findings from Ghuman et al (2006) demonstrate the importance of pre-school nutritional status (using height-for-age z-scores and hemoglobin levels) for child enrollment in first grade. Using similar assumptions as Alderman et al (2001), they instrument endogenous child nutritional status with characteristics of day care centers in villages where children lived prior to elementary age. They find that childhood nutrition has a significant and positive impact on school enrollment, but in contrast with Alderman et al, their instrumental variables estimates suggest upward bias in parameters produced by OLS.[8]

Another strategy is used both in Alderman et al (2006) and Glewwe et al (2001). These two papers share a similar assumption that child nutritional status is correlated with two important (unobserved) factors that also affect child schooling performance: (i) the *home environment* provided by a parent and affecting school performance; and (ii) the child's *health endowment*, which affects how a child performs relative to others in school. To deal with these unobservables, they combine household (maternal) fixed-effect and instrumental

---

to affect current period household welfare, which would further complicate estimation of the childhood effect. We consider this issue further in our empirical discussion of our instrumental variables below.

[8] The inconsistency might be caused by weak instruments bias. As indicated in their results, F-statistics for their excluded instrumental variable instrumental variable is only significant at 10% level and it is not clear whether the results are robust to weak instruments bias.

variables estimation techniques. Alderman et al (2006) use negative shocks (from war and drought) that affected children of preschool age to instrument for child nutritional status. They find that better preschool nutritional status is associated with more completed years of schooling. Glewwe et al (2001) use height-for-age for older siblings and differenced month of birth dummy variables as instrumental variables. They find that undernourished children entered school later and performed more poorly on cognitive achievement tests relative to better-nourished children.

This paper has two objectives. First, we add to the existing literature examining the relationship between early childhood nutrition and subsequent child schooling using a unique dataset collected in Indonesia. In common with the four studies discussed above, we use an instrumental variable technique to estimate the effect of childhood nutrition on the probability of delayed enrollment or repeated grade. We use rainfall shocks occurring *in utero* for sampled children along with other household and community variables to identify children's nutritional status during pre-school age. We argue that shocks experienced prior to birth are relevant for determining both height-for-age z-scores and stunting as measures of long-term malnutrition. Contemporaneous shocks, such as price shocks, are unlikely to generate an appreciable effect on long-term measures of nutritional status such as height-for-age z-scores.

In addition, as health and nutritional status may as well be affected by government policy as well as parental choice and health shocks affecting the innate healthiness of children (Glewwe 2005), we evaluate how exposure to community-based health service providers during early childhood affected the influence of health status on educational outcomes. In particular, we examine whether exposure to village midwives alleviates the effect of low early nutritional status in early childhood on subsequent school enrollment, or alternatively, whether presence of midwives complements the benefits of early nutritional status for school enrollment. At present, there are few studies that directly link past experience of malnutrition, exposure to public health programs and subsequent socio-economic outcomes.

Results of our analysis have important policy implications regardless of the estimated effect. Presence of a village midwife may reduce the effects of negative shocks to early childhood nutrition on subsequent school outcomes and assist with recovery from the effects of shocks to health status during early childhood. Alternatively, if midwives simply complement the effects of good health status, then they may still be playing an important role in maintaining health status and facilitating school enrollment, but this result would underline the importance of finding other means to support early childhood nutritional status. We use presence of a village midwife in the community when children were of pre-school age to represent child exposure to community-based health services, and interact this indicator with our measure of childhood nutrition. We then include community dummy variables in this intent-to-treat approach to control for features of the community correlated with placement of a midwife.

This approach allows us to identify how presence of a midwife influences the effect of early childhood nutrition on subsequent enrollment while avoiding bias from endogenous placement of a midwife in the village.

Our analysis examines another dimension along which village midwives may play an important role for influencing outcomes. Earlier studies demonstrated the important role played by village midwives in improving the health of prime age women (Frankenberg and Thomas 2001) and of pre-school age children (Frankenberg et al 2005).[9] We argue that if there is link from childhood nutrition to child schooling, then the presence of a public health program that improved child health could also have an important impact on child-schooling.

Our analyses make use of panel data from three waves Indonesia Family Life Survey (IFLS). This ongoing survey provides a rich source of information on individuals and households, as well as their access to facilities and the characteristics of the communities where they reside. In particular, we will link the childhood nutritional status of children between 6-59 months in 1993 with their schooling in 1997 (for an older group, who were 3 to 4 years old in 1993) and in 2000 (for a younger group, who were up to 2 years of age in 1993). We further link sampled children with presence of a midwife in the community where they lived in 1993 to evaluate how exposure to a village midwife prior to

---

[9]Extensive discussions of the village midwife program can also be found in Frankenberg and Thomas (2001)

five years of age interacted with early childhood nutrition influenced school enrollment. In order to identify nutritional status, we also exploit historical rainfall data (Kirono, 2000, and Kirono et al, 1999) from the month and year when the sampled children were conceived.

Our results show that childhood nutritional status reduced the probability of delayed enrollment, but not the probability of repeating a grade. The effect of childhood nutrition on subsequent schooling is greater for boys than for girls. Our preferred specifications produce estimates that are 5 to 7 times larger than when estimates ignore the endogeneity of childhood nutrition. In addition, we find that presence of a village midwife in the community in fact magnifies the effect childhood nutrition on child schooling implying that a village midwife complements nutritional status in early childhood. We also perform simulations to show the likely effects of increasing the share of communities with midwives. The result shows further improvement in the role of child health and nutrition in improving child schooling. This implies that exposure to village midwife, particularly during childhood, might be used as policy instrument to reduce gap in child schooling through improvement of child health and nutrition.

This paper thus contributes to the literature on impacts of early childhood nutrition in two significant ways. First, this study adds to existing studies which control for the endogeneity of childhood nutrition when estimating its impact on child schooling. In particular, we utilize exogenous rainfall shocks as source of identification for nutritional status during childhood. Second, we examine how

14

placing health service providers in Indonesian communities affects the relationship between early childhood nutritional status and subsequent schooling outcomes. We thus estimate whether the importance of early childhood nutrition status for subsequent school enrollment is affected by presence of community based health service providers. Our results provide an indication of how presence of health providers may interact with child health status to improve schooling outcomes.

The remaining of the paper is organized as follows. In section 2, we provide a simple framework to explain analytically how childhood nutrition may affect child schooling conditional on other variables. We also show how government policy may determine child schooling through a change in health, health environment and health prices. In section 3, we propose an empirical model and strategy to identify the effect of early childhood nutrition on schooling, and then extend our discussion to examine how presence of a village midwife interacts with early childhood nutrition to affect child schooling. We next discuss data, the community setting, and concerns with the data in section 4. In section 5, we present and discuss our results and conclude in section 6.

2.2. Analytical Framework

This section presents a simple analytical framework to model the relationship between past child nutritional status, availability of a health service provider and child schooling.[10] We adopt a two-period analytical framework developed by Glewwe (2005, 2007). The first period is a preschool stage in which children are younger than 5 years of age. Clinical nutritionists argue that this period, and in particular the period between 6 and 24 months, is when nutritional interventions and supplemental feeding are likely to have the greatest impact on subsequent child biological and cognitive development. If parents and the health service provider have knowledge of this relationship, we expect greater investment in child health during the period. The second period occurs when children are of primary school age, or age 5 and older. During this period, and conditional on child health and nutritional status, parents and government invest in child education, and achievements in schooling may be related to child nutritional status in the first period.

We start with production function for child schooling in period two which is specified as a function of child and parent characteristics during both periods one and two:

$$S_2 = A(H_1, H_2, EI_1, EI_2, \phi, SC) \qquad (1)$$

where S is a child schooling outcome, H represents health and nutritional status during period i (i=1,2), EI is (parental) education input at period i (i=1,2), ϕ is (unobserved) innate child ability (e.g., intelligence, motivation), and SC are

_____

[10]Our discussion in this section draws inspiration from Glewwe (2005).

school characteristics. Equation (1) focuses on assessing the role of child nutritional status on child schooling while holding other factors constant. This relationship is expressed as a structural equation since it only includes variables that measure direct effects of each right hand side variable on child education.

Academic achievement, as highlighted by (1), is important but not our main object of analysis. It is difficult to estimate because child academic attainment and some other factors such as EI are endogenous as they are under the control of parents and thus reflect parental preferences toward children's education as well as health.[11] School characteristic, SC, are also potentially endogenous since parents can choose the school their children attend and the government can decide by how much to invest in school quality. In addition, other important factors, such as child innate ability and school inputs, are unobserved. Our objective here is to evaluate the effect of child nutritional status and health policy on child schooling using conditional demand functions for child education. By estimating conditional demand, we avoid some of the complications arising when estimating the effect of childhood nutrition on child schooling using the schooling production function described above.

We derive the conditional demand function for child education by first substituting the endogenous independent variables, other than nutritional status,

---

[11] Assuming that household face resources constraint, allocating resources toward educational inputs should affect those toward children's health inputs.

with relevant exogenous variables. The reduced-forms for the education inputs *EI* in each period i *(i=1,2)* are specified as:[12]

$$EI_1 = ei_1(Y, Med, Fed, PS, \sigma, \alpha; PH_1, HE_1, \tau, \eta) \qquad (2)$$

$$EI_2 = ei_2(H_1, Y, Med, Fed, PS, \sigma, \alpha; PH_2, HE_2, \tau, \eta) \qquad (3)$$

where Y is parental income, *Med* and *Fed* are mother and father education, respectively, *PS* are prices of schooling and educational inputs, σ is parental preference toward child schooling, *PH* are prices for health in each period i *(i=1,2)*, *HE* is health environment, τ is parents' preferences toward child health, and η is the innate healthiness of the child.

We next substitute equations (2) and (3) into equation (1) to yield the conditional demand function for child schooling as:

$$S_2 = a_{CD}(H_1, H_2, Y, Med, Fed, PS, SC, \sigma, \alpha; PH_1, PH_2, HE_1, HE_2, \tau, \eta) \qquad (4)$$

---

[12] As discussed in Glewwe (2005), one complication arises when specifying the reduced form for child educational inputs: it is reasonable that child health and nutritional status may enter into parent decisions about the education inputs of their children. This creates a problem particularly since current health status is endogenous. To avoid this complication, researchers sometimes use previous period health status in current period reduced form education demand functions to avoid this complication.

18

This function is still not fully in reduced form because it includes current nutritional status as an endogenous variable in addition to exogenous variables. This specification picks up the direct impact of changes in health status (as in equation 1) as well as an indirect effect when change in health affects other variables before the impact on change in child schooling, S. For example part of the impact of good health in period 1 operates indirectly through parental education input in period 2, as parents respond to health status by increasing or decreasing their inputs into child education.

In addition, equation (4) can also be used to identify the impact of government policies in health and education on child schooling. The impact of health policy can be characterized as a change in either health prices (PH) or health environment (HE). In particular, the impact of health policy is channeled through two pathways. First, a health pathway includes the direct impact of child health on children cognitive development through equation (1), and indirect impacts of (lagged) child health on parental education inputs through equations (2) and (3). Secondly, there is a reallocation pathway through which substitution and income effects of PH and HE influence parental education through equations (2) and (3).

2.3. Empirical Model and Identification

We first focus on estimating the effect of childhood nutritional status on subsequent child schooling. Our empirical model of the conditional demand for child schooling is represented by a dynamic model of the impact of nutrition on subsequent schooling:[13]

$$S_{2i} = \alpha + \beta H_{1i} + \delta'\mathbf{X}_{2i} + \gamma'P_{2h} + \lambda'\mathbf{Z}_{2c} + v_{2i} \qquad (5)$$

where S is child schooling, H is nutritional status in period one when children are 5 years old or younger, X is vector of household characteristics (including, among others, income, mother's education and father's education), P is a vector of prices, Z is a vector of community characteristics, which might have an effect on child school enrollment, and v is a disturbance term. Numbers in subscript indicate period of realization for each variable. While letters in subscript, i, h and c, each indicate individual, household or community level variables.

As discussed in the previous section, current health status is supposed to be included in equation 5. Our primary interest in equation 5, however, is to measure the impact of early childhood nutritional status on subsequent schooling outcomes. To do so, we need to exclude the current health status from the schooling outcomes equation as we assume that the impact of past nutritional status on current schooling is through current health status. Otherwise the

---

[13] For our conditional demand for child schooling to be consistent with equation 4, we should include current nutritional status in the empirical model shown in equation 5. As discussed by Behrman and Lavy (1998) and Alderman et al (2001) the coefficient on current health status in relation to child schooling is difficult to interpret as the estimated impact of current health on current child schooling. We therefore dropped current health status from right hand side of equation 5 and focus on estimating the impact of previous period (period 1) nutritional status on current (period 2) child schooling. Our identification strategy must be robust to potential biases introduced by unobserved nutritional status.

impact of past nutritional status on schooling will be absorbed by current health status. In addition, including current health status in the schooling outcomes equation introduces another endogeneity problem when estimating equation 5.

Estimating equation 5 with OLS is likely to produce bias in parameter β as nutritional health status in period 1 is correlated with unobserved time-invariant innate child health as well as parent preferences toward child health captured in v. Some studies such as Alderman et al (2006), Glewwe and King (2001) combine maternal-household fixed-effects with instrumental variable techniques to address unobserved heterogeneity at parent (household) and individual levels. Alternatively, as discussed in Glewwe et al (2001) and Alderman et al (2001), if we can find shocks (price or weather) that (i) are of sufficient magnitude to affect child stature but not their siblings, (ii) vary sufficiently across households (or even individuals), we can use such shocks to identify childhood height-for-age as it addresses unobserved heterogeneity at both individual and household levels.

We follow an identification strategy similar to that of Alderman et al (2001) and Alderman et al (2009), but differ with them in our choice of the timing of shocks during childhood used to identify childhood nutrition. We argue that price shocks that were measured contemporaneously with early child nutrition indicator may not be sufficient for explaining the child height –which is used to measure early childhood malnutrition. This is because any type of shock, will likely take considerable time to be reflected in child height. Alderman et al (2001) acknowledge this concern although argue that as long as such (contemporaneous) price shocks are still partially correlated with childhood nutritional status, we can still use them to identify endogenous childhood nutrition.

We make use of long-term historical rainfall data, and use *in utero* rainfall shocks, particularly those during the mother's second and third trimester of pregnancy, and interact them with child age (in months) when height was measured. The interaction between *in utero* rainfall shocks and child age is employed to improve the instruments' power in identifying child nutritional status by exploiting the length of time from the occurrence of the shocks to the time when child height was measured in 1993. The identifying assumption is that *in utero* rainfall shocks and time to the period when height was measured have no impact on subsequent child schooling except through childhood nutrition. In addition, we also include the value of total household assets, the height of father and mother and interactions of number of *posyandu* and child age, all measured in period 1, as additional excluded instruments.

There are a few potential concerns with these instruments. First, past rainfall shocks might have had large enough magnitudes to have long term impacts on household assets or consumption which thus directly affects child schooling. Alternatively, prior rainfall shocks might have led to disasters, such as floods that adversely affected long term household access to education facilities and thus also to later child schooling. Such concerns, if not addressed, would cast doubt on the validity of the instruments. To deal with concerns about affects

22

on wealth, we control for per-capita expenditure measure and include a village dummy in the second stage regression so the effect of past rainfall shocks on education, through household wealth, would be indirect and operating through these variables. Similarly, one might be concerned that parents' height (from period 1) should not be in excluded instruments as they might affect subsequent child education. But we argue that the effect of parents' height on child education would be conditional on child health. Thus, including a child height indicator in the second stage regression should take care of this concern.

In addition, as the model suggests, prices and some community level variables also determine child schooling outcomes. So we include in the equation some food prices and community-level fixed effects. We argue that after implementing this procedure, H_{1i} is no longer correlated with omitted variables in error term and thus β is unbiased estimator of the impact of childhood nutritional status on primary school enrollment.

We then seek to evaluate the effect of presence of midwife in the community during childhood in the same schooling outcomes conditional on past nutritional status. Our approach is to estimate intent-to-treat effect of the village midwife. The important role of midwives has been identified for several outcomes such as womens health (Frankenberg and Thomas 2001) and young child nutritional status (Frankenberg et al 2005). Nevertheless none of previous studies have examined how exposure to community-based health service providers, such as midwives, might interact with early childhood nutritional status to affect child schooling outcomes. We attempt to establish a potential link between exposure to a village midwife when children are still young (under 5 years old) and subsequent enrollment when of school age. Specifically, we are interested in how exposure to a midwife interacts with nutritional health status in early childhood. Exposure to midwife might reduce the negative effect of past malnutrition on subsequent school enrollment if village midwives provide health services that compensate for *in utero* shocks affecting nutritional health status. Alternatively, we may find that presence of a midwife reinforces the benefits of better early childhood nutritional status. We thus want to estimate the following equation:

$$S_{2t} = \alpha + T + \beta_1 H_{1t} + \beta_2 Mid_{1c}^{93} + \beta_3 H_{1t} * Mid_{1c}^{93} + \delta' \mathbf{X}_{2t} + \gamma' \mathbf{S}_{2t} + v_{2t} \qquad (6)$$

where Mid^{93} is an indicator for a presence of midwife in the community where a child resided in period 1, or when they were of pre-school age (in 1993). We estimate equation (2) using instrumental variables methods by employing shocks at the early age of life as instruments for early childhood nutritional status. In addition to those we discussed when estimating equation 5, one concern is that presence of midwife in period 1 is likely to be correlated with some omitted variable, such as availability of education facilities within the community, that

24

might affect subsequent school enrollment.[14] If this is true, ignoring such correlation will lead to bias in the parameter of interest. We thus include a fixed community effect, μ_c , and rewrite (6) as below:

$$S_{2i} = \alpha + T + \beta_1 H_{1i} + \beta_2 H_{1i} * Mid_{1c}^{93} + \delta' X_{2i} + \gamma' S_{2i} + \mu_c + v_{2i} \qquad (7)$$

Note that when we include μ_c to control for (potential) endogenous midwife placement, the midwife dummy can no longer be included directly as it will be perfectly collinear with the village fixed effect. By controlling for community fixed-effects, we control for endogenous placement of midwives by 1993. Community fixed-effects are also useful as they control for unobserved elementary school characteristics as we assume that the sampled children would go to the closest school to the community.[15] In this way we assume those schools' characteristics are fixed across periods.[16]

The exclusion of a midwife variable due to inclusion of a community fixed-effect means that we will not be able to estimate the direct effect of midwife on schooling outcomes. Fortunately that is not our main interest. Instead we would like to see how exposure to a midwife affects the schooling outcomes through early childhood nutritional status. To do so, we will focus on the

---

[14] For example, Pitt et al (1993) find that the presence of one type of facilities was correlated with another type of facilities.

[15] Although IFLS interviews elementary schools, it is not possible to link every child in the sample to the school he or she attended without making arbitrary assumptions.

[16] The use of community fixed-effect here also implies that we should focus only on the children that lived in panel communities during the observed periods.

interaction between early childhood height-for-age and dummy variable for the presence of a midwife in community during period when child was in pre-school age.

2.4. Data and sample setting

This study uses three waves of panel data from Indonesia Family Life Survey (IFLS) 1993, 1997 and 2000. IFLS is a panel survey which collected very rich socio-economic information on many aspects of individual lives and households as well about characteristics of communities where those individuals and households resided. The detail description about sampling in each of the three survey waves is provided in Strauss et al (2004), Frankenberg and Thomas (2000), and Frankenberg et al (1995), respectively.

Our sample in this study includes children who were between 6 and 59 month in 1993 (born between 1988 and 1993) and have their height (or length) measured in the 1993 survey. We then link the 1993 measured nutritional status for children who were born between 1988 and 1990 (with their enrollment status in 1997 and for those who were born from 1991 to 1993 with their primary school enrollment in 2000 then pool those two data files. In this set up, we thus examine the impact of early childhood nutritional status on schooling of children who were between 7-9 years of age in 1997 and 2000. The IFLS data also allow us to identify how midwife exposure, when the children were 5 years old or younger, interacts with early childhood nutrition in affecting enrollment. As mentioned above, we expect that the exposure to midwife health services during such an early age might either reduce the negative effect of malnutrition during childhood, or alternatively complement the health endowment of children who were not suffering from malnutrition.

Historical rainfall data are obtained from Kirono (2000) and Kirono et al (1999) which collect rainfall from 62 weather stations across Indonesia from 1960 to 1999. For our purpose, we use calculate shocks using rainfall data from the entire period spanning 1960 to 1993, and then calculate shocks for the period when our sampled children were born. From the data, we generate monthly rainfall shocks which we define as monthly rainfall deviations from long-term monthly rainfall trends and presented as monthly shocks.

The summary statistics of key variables are in table 1 below. All variables are measured in period 2 (1997 and 2000 surveys, pooled) except for two main variables of interest, nutritional status and presence of midwife in the community, and instrumental variables that are measured in period 1 (1993 survey). We look at two child schooling measures, whether child experienced delayed enrollment when they entered primary school and whether they ever repeated a grade, both are expressed as binary dummy variables.[17] There are 18 and 10 percent of children who experienced delayed enrollment and repeated classes respectively.

---

[17] For Indonesia, the two indicators appear to be important measures for primary education particularly after reaching near universal enrollment for primary education.

For measures of nutritional status (measured by height-for-age) we use (continuous) height-for-age z-score and (binary) whether a child was non-stunted which is a measure of child malnutrition.[18] The health literature has suggested height (or length for baby and infant) is an indicator with less measurement error for child health and nutritional status relative to the other health measures.[19] More importantly, the use of height-for-age will fit with the focus of this study that investigates the long-term relationship between early childhood nutrition to subsequent child schooling. The 1993 IFLS data show that children younger than 5 of age have heights that are on average 1.39 standard deviations lower than those of children with similar age and gender in US. Meanwhile nearly 29 percent of children in the 1993 sample were exposed to village midwives.

We also control for other covariates that may affect the household decision to send children to elementary school and in part might represent parent preferences for child education, the home study environment and the intrahousehold allocation process. We control for parents' education, age of household head, household composition, and per capita expenditure. In addition, as the model suggests, we also include current price for some food items (rice, sugar, cooking oil and condensed milk). We also include a time dummy to control for any secular trend across two different periods of life (1 for

---

[18] Stunted is defined when child height-for-age z-score is less than negative 2.
[19] In IFLS, height and weight are measured by special trained health workers with regularly calibrated health equipment. For this reason, we believe that measurement error is negligible in this case.

school age period, 0 otherwise). The mean and standard deviation for each of these variables are presented in table 1.

2.5. Results

In this section we present and discuss the results. We first focus on the impact of childhood nutritional status on subsequent child schooling outcomes. The results, consistent with some previous studies, show that childhood nutrition matter in determining subsequent child schooling. Our preferred estimates also indicate stronger effect of childhood nutrition on subsequent schooling implying biased results when correlation between nutritional status and omitted variables captured in error term are ignored. We then try to seek potential effect of the presence of village midwife in the community where those children resided when they were in pre-school age. In particular, we are interested in whether such exposure might reduce the negative effects of malnutrition which occurred earlier in childhood.

2.5.1. Impact of early childhood nutritional status on child schooling

We estimate equation 5 and firstly ignore the correlation of childhood nutritional status with unobserved heterogeneity such as child health endowment and parent preferences for child quality. The result in table 2 and shows that improved childhood nutrition lowers the probability of a child experiencing delayed enrollment. The size of the coefficient when not controlling for community fixed-effect suggests that an increase in child height-for-age by one standard deviation lowered the probability of delayed enrollment by 3.2 percent. When controlling for community fixed-effects, the effect became slightly stronger, where an increase in child height-for-age by one standard deviation reduced the probability of delayed enrollment by 3.5 percent. The effect of other covariates appears to be consistent with literature on determinants of child schooling. Increasing parent, and in particular father's education, reduces the probability of delayed enrollment. Per capita expenditure is also significant and has a negative sign as one would expect. Household composition variables are also important for child schooling but with different signs of influence on child schooling. Number of children (age 6-14 years old) residingin the household has the disadvantaged of delaying primary school enrollment. This might imply that there is competition among for household educational resources. In addition, number of male adults (age 15-59 years old) in the family reduces the probability of a child experiencing delayed enrollment, but this occurs only when we are not controlling for community fixed-effects.

Using a dummy indicator for stunting provides further support for our findings. Suffering from stunting makes the probability of delayed enrolment increase by 8 or 9 percent depending on whether we control for community fixed-effects. Other covariates show similar direction of influence on child delayed enrollment compared to when we do not control for the community fixed-effect.

Table 3 shows result from estimating childhood nutrition on probability of repeating grade using a model that fails to control for endogenous health status. Estimation results for each outcome using different specifications (with and without community fixed-effects) show insignificant and inconsistent sign of childhood nutrition effect on probability of grade repetition. Some other covariates however remain significant with consistent sign as in the previous estimation.

Although the sign of the parameters of interest appear to be consistent with theoretical model, the estimations using treating health status as exogenous will be biased for the reasons we discussed earlier. Behrman and Lavy (1998) note that the direction of the bias from this naïve model, whether upward or downward, depend on the nature of intrahousehold allocation process. To address this issue, we adopt instrumental variable technique in estimating the effect of early childhood nutrition on child schooling.

We first examine effects of early childhood nutrition on probability of delayed enrollment and present results in Table 4. We first look at the bottom panel of table 4 where some statistical test results for instrumental variables are provided. The tests are conducted both for measures of childhood nutritional status, height-for-age and stunting status, and each are conducted for specifications with and without community fixed-effects. As we see, the F-test for excluded instruments for both endogenous regressors, height-for-age and stunting status, produce a significant statistic at the 1 percent confidence level.

31

Recent econometrics literature on instrumental variables suggests that these test statistics are not sufficient. Weak instrument bias may be present when there is non-zero but small correlation between endogenous regressors and excluded instruments although F-statistics of the excluded instruments are significant.[20]

We thus perform additional tests which include: (i) Kleibergen-Paap rk LM statistics, to test the relevance of the excluded instruments on the endogenous regressors (under Ho: equation is underidentified), and (ii) Hansen J statistics which test over-identifying restriction (under joint null hypothesis that the excluded instruments are valid). These tests show that the excluded instruments are strong and valid for the endogenous regressors whether or not we control for community fixed-effect in the equation. We also present the first stage regression results in the appendices.

Results from estimating the impact of childhood nutrition on child schooling using 2SLS are in top panel of table 4 (delayed enrollment) and table 5 (grade repetition). We start with the effect of childhood nutrition on delayed enrollment in table 4. In terms of the direction of the influence, the effects of childhood nutrition from 2SLS estimation are mostly consistent with results shown in table 2. With few exceptions, other covariates are also consistent with those in table 2. Controlling for endogeneity in childhood nutritional status makes the effect of early childhood nutrition on probability of delayed

---

[20] see Wooldidge (2002) for theoretical implications for this problem and Bhaum et al (2003, 2007) for practical strategy to deal with this.

enrollment stronger, implying downward bias in the parameter estimated using OLS.

Without controlling for community fixed-effects, an increase in childhood height-for-age by 1 standard deviation lowered probability of delayed enrollment by 9.7 percent (column 1). Non-stunted children are 31.3 percent less likely to experience delayed enrollment relative to stunted children (column 3). However results from this specification may still be biased if there is omitted heterogeneity at the village level, including school characteristics that are likely correlated with child schooling. It is also possible that school access and quality differ across cohorts, particularly as the 1997/1998 economic crisis may have led to deterioration in the quality of schools. To handle these issues, we include community fixed-effects in the IV model.

As shown column 2 of table 4, the effect of controlling for community fixed-effects makes the effect of childhood nutrition on child schooling even stronger. An increase in child height-for-age in period 1 by 1 standard deviation reduced the probability of delayed enrollment by 15.8 percent. In addition, non-stunted children are more likely to avoid delayed enrollment relative to stunted child by about 54 percent. As we have addressed most of potential problems, these results, we argue, are relatively unbiased compared to those from models failing to control for endogeneity of childhood nutritional status and community fixed-effects.

When using grade repetition as the school outcome, we also find a negative sign of the effect childhood nutritional status on probability of repeating grade (table 5), we fail to reject the null hypotheses that the effect of childhood nutrition equals to zero. As this is consistent with the result from OLS estimation in table 3, one possible explanation why we found no childhood nutrition effect is that grade repetition is rare (the mean sample value of grade repetition is 9.6 percent). This probably occurs because we use young school age children who were 7-9 years old by the time we observe their schooling outcome and therefore the occurrence of grade repetition was not as high as for older children.

We next examine whether the effect of childhood nutrition on subsequent child schooling differs between boys and girls. We focus on delayed enrollment outcomes as we do not see significant effect of childhood nutrition on grade repetition. The results are presented in table 6.

As we can see in the bottom panel of table 6, F-statistics of excluded instruments are lower than 10 although they still maintain significance at the 1 percent level. To address concern over the possibility of weak instruments, we estimate the effect of childhood nutrition on delayed enrollment based on gender using instrumental variable-limited information maximum likelihood (IV-LIML). Baum et al (2007) show that IV-LIML estimation is robust in the presence of weak instrument.

Result in table 6 shows that childhood nutrition mattered for boys more than girls. Particularly 1 standard deviation increase in height-for-age z-score lowers probability of delayed enrollment by 21.3 percent for boys compared to 12.4 percent for girls. Using an extreme measure of malnutrition, non-stunted boys have 66.1 percent chance of enrolling on time relative to stunted boys. For girls, being non-stunted improves probability of enrolling on time by 42.7 percent relative to stunted girls.

These results therefore suggest the importance of childhood nutrition for child school enrollment decisions when they about to reach school age, but not for child grade repetition. These are consistent with previous findings and therefore reinforce the need for investment and intervention to prevent malnutrition at a very young age. Consistent with previous studies (see Alderman 2001, Behrman dan Lavy 1998, Glewwe et al 2000, and Glewwe and King 2001), the results also show that the estimated effect generated by OLS may suffer a substantial bias and which may mislead policy makers in addressing the problems related to early childhood malnutrition.

2.5.2. Impact of presence of midwife during early childhood on schooling

Knowing the importance of early childhood health and nutritional status in lowering on child schooling, we then asked whether the presence of a midwife during such critical period of age helped children when they reached school-age. The link that we try to establish between past exposure to public health program and later schooling outcomes is built on the previous findings that the presence of village midwife increased health of young children (Frankenberg et al 2005). Therefore if the presence of village midwife improved child health (as measured by height-for-age), then we may expect that such a program may also yield improvements in child schooling outcomes conditional on improvements in child health.

Identifying an effect of the village midwife is not straightforward. One might believe that presence of a midwife in period one (when child is in early age) is exogenous for education measured in period 2 (when child is in school age). However, as shown in Pitt et al (2003), placement of a public program is likely to be correlated with the presence of other programs that already exist (and remained) in the community. In our case, placement of public programs might be correlated with availability or quality of school or other education programs which in turn might affect parent decisions on investment in child education.[21] We thus argue that controlling for community fixed-effects is important in this case and this should address correlation between the placement of a midwife with time-invariant omitted heterogeneity including the presence of other public programs in the community.

As we previously mentioned, however, there is a cost of including community fixed-effect. As we seek to evaluate the intent-to-treat effect of

---

[21]Using Indonesia SUSENAS data, Pitt et al (2001) show that the placement of public programs was correlated with the presence of another program that already existed and the effect of the program is sensitive to whether or not one controls for this correlation.

presence of midwife, the inclusion of community fixed-effect will absorb all fixed community level effects including presence of a midwife. We thus identify the midwife effect by calculating the partial effect of childhood nutritional status when presence of midwife is explicitly controlled for in the equation and compare it with the one from equation without control of presence of midwife. The difference is attributed to the presence of midwife in the community in period 1. If presence of midwife indeed helps schooling of children given their childhood nutritional status, then we will see that the presence of midwife will increase the partial effect of childhood nutrition on subsequent schooling outcomes.

We focus on the specifications that control for community fixed-effect in column 2 and 4 of table 8. As we expect, the midwife variable is dropped by the inclusion of community variable and the sign of childhood nutrition (for both height-for-age z-score and non-stunted status) are negative. The effect of childhood nutrition is significant at the 1 percent level where the size of the effects are -0.155 (height-for-age z-score) and -0.507 (dummy for non-stunted). Interactions between childhood nutritional status (both for height-for-age z-score and dummy for non-stunted) and midwife are insignificant.

In the presence of an interaction term, however, we should not only use individual statistical test to evaluate the partial effect of parameter of interest. Instead, as noted in Wooldridge (2003), we need to conduct joint significant test for height-for-age and interaction of height-for-age and midwife. The F-statistics show that childhood nutrition variables and interactions with midwife are significant at 1 percent level as shown in bottom panel of column 2 and 4 of table 8.

We thus calculate the partial effect of childhood nutrition in the presence of a midwife and present the result in table 8A. We first look at the effect by using height-for-age z-score as a measure of nutritional status. We find that the partial effect of height-for-age (at midwife sample mean, 0.287) is -0.166 which says that an increase in one standard deviation of child height lowered the probability of delayed enrollment by 16.6 percent which is higher than the effect when no midwife at all (15.5 percent).

Based on the estimated parameter in table 8, we also predict the effect of child height in cases where presence of midwife in the communities increased to 50 and 75 percent. When probability of a midwife in the community is increased to 50 percent, a one standard deviation increase in childhood nutritional status lowers the probability of delayed enrollment by 17.4 percent. While if presence of midwife is expanded further to 75 percent, the effect of childhood nutrition becomes even stronger where an increase in one standard deviation of child height lowers the probability of delayed enrollment by 18.4 percent.

When using stunting status (column 2 of table 8A), the partial effect of childhood nutrition in the presence of midwife (sample mean=0.287) is -0.553. This suggests that by being not stunted during childhood, the probability a child enrolls in school on time is 55.7 percent higher than if he (or she) suffered stunting during childhood. Recall that when we do not explicitly control for presence of a midwife, eliminating stunting during early childhood could reduce the probability of delayed enrollment by 50.7 percent relative to those who were stunted during childhood. Predicted effects of being not-stunted during childhood on probability of delayed enrollment by hypothetically increasing the probability of a midwife in the community to 50 and 75 percent are consistent with our calculation using height-for-age z-score as measure of childhood nutrition. When the presence of a midwife is increased to 50 (75) percent, the importance of not being stunted during childhood is even higher. Non-stunted children are 38.7 (62.7) percent more likely to be enrolled in school at age 7, and this is 58.7(62.7) percent higher than if they had experienced stunting during early childhood.

We next turn to table 9 where we estimate the effect childhood nutrition in the presence of midwife on probability of repeating a grade. As in table 8, we again focus on the specifications that include community fixed-effects to control for potential endogenous placement of a village midwife. We first find that childhood nutritional status does not have an effect on probability of repeating a grade as none of coefficients for height-for-age z-score and dummy for non-stunted are significant. The join significant test for childhood nutrition (for both height-for-age and dummy of non-stunted) and its interactions with dummy for midwife presence indicate that they jointly are not significantly different from zero. This is consistent with result in table 5 which shows no significant effect of childhood nutrition on probability of repeating a grade.

Coefficients for interaction between childhood nutrition and dummy for presence of midwife, however, are negative and significant at 5 and 10 percent level. Coefficients for interaction between dummy for presence of midwife and height-for-age z-score is -0.073 (column 2), while for its interaction with dummy for not-stunted is 0.333 (column 4). What do these coefficients suggest? As the effect of childhood nutritional status on probability of repeating a grade is statistically zero (as also indicated in table 5), the significant interaction coefficients (between childhood nutrition and midwife) indicate the effect of presence of a midwife. It suggests that an increase in one standard deviation in child height among children exposed to a midwife will reduce the probability of repeating a grade by 7.3 percent relative to those who live in community without village midwife (column 2 of table 9). It also that being well nourished in a community with village midwife lowers the probability of repeating a grade by 33.3 relative to other children in the sample area.

2.6. Conclusions

This study evaluates the impact of childhood nutritional status and the presence of a public health program on subsequent child schooling in Indonesia during 1990s. Guided by the model, we estimate dynamic relationship of childhood nutrition and subsequent child schooling in which we carefully address the potential correlation between childhood nutrition and important but unobserved factors such as child innate healthiness and parents' taste toward child quality. In addition, with access to long-term historical rainfall data, we create rainfall shocks during conception period and use them to identify childhood nutritional status. By controlling for endogenous nutritional status, we find that reducing incidence of poor childhood nutrition reduces also the probability of delayed enrollment, but not the probability of repeating a grade. More importantly, the estimated effects when taking into account the endogeneity of childhood nutrition are 5-7 times stronger than when ignoring the endogeneity of childhood nutrition.

The effect of childhood nutrition on subsequent child schooling is even higher if child has access to public health facilities. Looking particularly at presence of midwife, we find that the presence of midwife magnifying the effect of childhood nutritional status on subsequent child schooling. This result suggests positive effect of presence of midwife on child schooling.

What does this result imply? From the policy perspective, this result reinforces the importance of investment on nutritional status of children at very young ages, even just after conception and before birth. One effective channel of health investment, as this study suggests, can be through local public health facilities such as village midwife. From a methodological perspective, the results presented in this study highlight the importance of taking into account the endogeneity in childhood nutrition and other estimation issues when estimating

its effect on subsequent child schooling.

Table 2.1. Descriptive statistics of main variables

Variable	Mean	Std. Dev.
Delayed enrollment (Yes=1)	0.146	0.353
Ever repeated grade (Yes=1)	0.096	0.295
Heigh-for-age z-score (haz), lagged	-1.390	1.442
Presence of village midwife, lagged	0.287	0.453
Mother education (years)	4.205	5.505
Father education (years)	5.057	5.782
Household head age (years)	42.285	9.911
# of children (5-14 yo) in household	1.960	0.945
# of female adult (15-59 yo) in household	1.382	0.706
# of male adult (15-59 yo) in household	1.284	0.801
Per capita expenditure (log)	11.992	0.712
Price of rice (log)	7.414	0.387
Price of sugar (log)	7.813	0.375
Price of cooking oil (log)	7.846	0.376
Price of condensed milk (log)	7.781	0.503

Notes: lagged variables are measured in period 1 (1993 survey).

Table 2.2. Impact of childhood nutrition on probability of delayed enrollment, OLS

Dep. Var: delayed enrollment	Measure of childhood nutrition			
	Height-for age z-score		Non-stunted (Yes=1)	
(Yes=1)	1	2	3	4
Childhood nutrition	-0.032***	-0.035***	-0.090***	-0.083***
	(0.006)	(0.007)	(0.018)	(0.020)
Time dummy	0.087**	0.096*	0.077*	0.090*
	(0.042)	(0.049)	(0.042)	(0.049)
Mother education	-0.003*	-0.001	-0.003*	-0.001
	(0.002)	(0.002)	(0.002)	(0.002)
Father education	-0.005***	-0.004**	-0.005***	-0.004**
	(0.002)	(0.002)	(0.002)	(0.002)
Age of head of household	0.001	0.001	0.001	0.001
	(0.001)	(0.001)	(0.001)	(0.001)
# 6-14 yo children in HH	0.030***	0.037***	0.031***	0.039***
	(0.009)	(0.010)	(0.009)	(0.010)
# female adults in HH	0.000	0.007	-0.002	0.006
	(0.012)	(0.014)	(0.012)	(0.014)
# male adults in HH	-0.027**	-0.015	-0.027**	-0.016
	(0.011)	(0.012)	(0.011)	(0.012)
Per-capita expenditure	-0.040***	-0.031**	-0.042***	-0.034**
	(0.012)	(0.015)	(0.012)	(0.015)
Price of rice	0.017	-0.02	0.016	-0.027
	(0.030)	(0.051)	(0.030)	(0.051)
Price of sugar	0.008	0.065	0.011	0.063
	(0.059)	(0.073)	(0.059)	(0.073)
Price of cooking oil	0.016	0.006	0.016	0.002
	(0.021)	(0.030)	(0.021)	(0.030)
Price of condensed milk	-0.082**	-0.138***	-0.080**	-0.133***
	(0.035)	(0.050)	(0.035)	(0.050)
Constant	0.822**	0.989*	0.838**	1.103**
	(0.413)	(0.515)	(0.413)	(0.515)
Community fixed-effect	No	Yes	No	Yes
R-squared	0.06	0.25	0.06	0.25
Observations	1944	1944	1944	1944

Notes: Dependent variable is whether child experienced delayed enrollment (yes=1). Robust standard error is in parenthesis. (***), (**), (*) respectively indicate significant at 1, 5 and 10 percent level.

Table 2.3. Impact of childhood nutrition on probability of repeating grade, OLS

Dep. Var: Repeated grade (Yes=1)	Measure of childhood nutrition			
	Height-for age z-score		Non-stunted (Yes=1)	
	1	2	3	4
Childhood nutrition	-0.004	0.001	-0.005	0.005
	(0.005)	(0.006)	(0.015)	(0.016)
Time dummy	0.043	0.049	0.041	0.049
	(0.036)	(0.043)	(0.036)	(0.043)
Mother education	-0.003**	-0.004**	-0.003**	-0.004**
	(0.002)	(0.002)	(0.002)	(0.002)
Father education	-0.003**	-0.002	-0.003**	-0.002
	(0.002)	(0.002)	(0.002)	(0.002)
Age of head of household	0.000	0.000	0.000	0.000
	(0.001)	(0.001)	(0.001)	(0.001)
# 6-14 yo children in HH	0.006	0.009	0.006	0.01
	(0.007)	(0.008)	(0.007)	(0.008)
# female adults in HH	0.001	0.007	0.001	0.007
	(0.010)	(0.011)	(0.010)	(0.011)
# male adults in HH	-0.003	0.003	-0.003	0.003
	(0.009)	(0.010)	(0.009)	(0.010)
Per-capita expenditure	-0.019**	-0.012	-0.020**	-0.012
	(0.008)	(0.010)	(0.008)	(0.010)
Price of rice	-0.026	0.024	-0.027	0.025
	(0.020)	(0.030)	(0.020)	(0.031)
Price of sugar	0.004	0.049	0.005	0.049
	(0.058)	(0.075)	(0.058)	(0.075)
Price of cooking oil	-0.012	-0.028	-0.012	-0.028
	(0.021)	(0.029)	(0.021)	(0.029)
Price of condensed milk	0.025	-0.039	0.025	-0.039
	(0.022)	(0.036)	(0.022)	(0.036)
Constant	0.391	0.183	0.397	0.18
	(0.355)	(0.455)	(0.355)	(0.456)
Community fixed-effect	No	Yes	No	Yes
R-squared	0.02	0.20	0.02	0.21
Observations	1944	1944	1944	1944

Notes: Dependent variable is dummy for child experienced repeated grade (yes=1). Robust standard error is in parenthesis. (***), (**), (*) respectively indicate significant at 1, 5 and 10 percent level.

Table 2.4. Impact of childhood nutrition on probability of delayed enrollment: 2SLS

| Dep. Var: delayed enrollment | Measure of childhood nutrition | | | |
| | Height-for age z-score | | Non-stunted (Yes=1) | |
(Yes=1)	1	2	3	4
Childhood nutrition	-0.097***	-0.158***	-0.313***	-0.539***
	(0.023)	(0.030)	(0.077)	(0.108)
Time dummy	0.140***	0.166***	0.115***	0.154***
	(0.046)	(0.058)	(0.045)	(0.059)
Mother education	-0.003	0.000	-0.002	0.000
	(0.002)	(0.002)	(0.002)	(0.002)
Father education	-0.005***	-0.003	-0.005***	-0.004*
	(0.002)	(0.002)	(0.002)	(0.002)
Age of head of household	0.001	0.001	0.001	0.002
	(0.001)	(0.001)	(0.001)	(0.001)
# 6-14 yo children in HH	0.022**	0.026**	0.024**	0.030**
	(0.010)	(0.012)	(0.010)	(0.013)
# female adults in HH	0.009	0.016	0.005	0.009
	(0.014)	(0.015)	(0.013)	(0.016)
# male adults in HH	-0.030**	-0.018	-0.030**	-0.026*
	(0.012)	(0.013)	(0.012)	(0.015)
Per-capita expenditure	-0.021	-0.011	-0.024*	-0.022
	(0.014)	(0.017)	(0.014)	(0.017)
Price of rice	0.011	-0.046	0.000	-0.09
	(0.033)	(0.065)	(0.033)	(0.067)
Price of sugar	-0.025	0.056	-0.023	0.038
	(0.062)	(0.081)	(0.061)	(0.085)
Price of cooking oil	0.02	0.043	0.025	0.034
	(0.022)	(0.034)	(0.023)	(0.035)
Price of condensed milk	-0.090**	-0.159***	-0.086**	-0.143**
	(0.037)	(0.058)	(0.037)	(0.060)
Community fixed-effect	No	Yes	No	Yes
F-stat on the excluded instrument	23.46	18.85	19.25	13.56
(p-value)	(0.000)	(0.000)	(0.000)	(0.000)
Kleibergen-Paap rk LM statistic	122.39	92.71	111.19	73.68
(p-value)	(0.000)	(0.000)	(0.000)	(0.000)
Hansen J stat	3.89	5.74	4.21	4.53
(p-value)	(0.566)	(0.361)	(0.518)	(0.477)
Observations	1910	1890	1910	1890

Notes: Dependent variable is lagged height-for-age z-score. Robust standard error is in parenthesis. (***), (**), (*) respectively indicate significant at 1, 5 and 10 percent level. Excluded IVs are: interaction rainfall shocks during second and third trimester of *in utero* period and child age (in months), total household assets (log), height of father and mother (cm), age of children (in months) and interaction between number of posyandu in the village and child age, all are in period 1. First-stage regression for lagged height-for-age and stunted are in table A1 and A2.

Table 2.5. Impact of childhood nutrition on probability of repeating grade: 2SLS

| Dep. Var: Repeated grade | Measure of childhood nutrition | | | |
| | Height-for age z-score | | Non-stunted (Yes=1) | |
(Yes=1)	1	2	3	4
Childhood nutrition	-0.026	-0.015	-0.091	-0.043
	(0.019)	(0.022)	(0.061)	(0.076)
Time dummy	0.052	0.055	0.046	0.053
	(0.039)	(0.045)	(0.038)	(0.044)
Mother education	-0.003*	-0.004**	-0.003	-0.004**
	(0.002)	(0.002)	(0.002)	(0.002)
Father education	-0.003**	-0.002	-0.003**	-0.002
	(0.001)	(0.002)	(0.001)	(0.002)
Age of head of household	0.000	0.000	0.000	0.000
	(0.001)	(0.001)	(0.001)	(0.001)
# 6-14 yo children in HH	0.002	0.007	0.002	0.008
	(0.008)	(0.009)	(0.008)	(0.009)
# female adults in HH	0.004	0.006	0.004	0.005
	(0.011)	(0.012)	(0.011)	(0.012)
# male adults in HH	-0.004	0.002	-0.004	0.001
	(0.009)	(0.010)	(0.009)	(0.010)
Per-capita expenditure	-0.013	-0.009	-0.013	-0.01
	(0.010)	(0.011)	(0.010)	(0.011)
Price of rice	-0.02	0.028	-0.024	0.024
	(0.026)	(0.040)	(0.026)	(0.040)
Price of sugar	-0.003	0.044	-0.003	0.043
	(0.060)	(0.077)	(0.059)	(0.077)
Price of cooking oil	-0.011	-0.026	-0.01	-0.027
	(0.022)	(0.030)	(0.022)	(0.030)
Price of condensed milk	0.023	-0.04	0.024	-0.039
	(0.022)	(0.036)	(0.022)	(0.036)
Community fixed-effect	No	Yes	No	Yes
F-stat on the excluded instrument	23.46	18.85	19.25	13.56
(p-value)	(0.000)	(0.000)	(0.000)	(0.000)
Kleibergen-Paap rk LM statistic	122.39	92.71	111.19	73.68
(p-value)	(0.000)	(0.000)	(0.000)	(0.000)
Hansen J stat	2.80	4.46	2.43	4.91
(p-value)	(0.730)	(0.485)	(0.788)	(0.427)
Observations	1910	1890	1910	1890

Notes: Dependent variable is (lagged) dummy for child was stunted during childhood. Robust standard errors are in parenthesis. (***), (**), (*) respectively indicate significant at 1, 5 and 10 percent level. Excluded IVs are: interaction rainfall shocks during second and third trimester of *in utero* period and child age (in months), total household assets (log), height of father and mother (cm), age of children (in months) and interaction between number of posyandu in the village and child age, all are in period 1. First-stage regression for lagged height-for-age and stunted are in table A1 and A2.

Table 2.6. Heterogeneity impact of childhood nutrition on probability of delayed enrollment across gender, 2SLS-LIML

| Dep. Var: delayed enrollment | Measure of childhood nutrition | | | |
| | Height-for age z-score | | Non-stunted (Yes=1) | |
(Yes=1)	Boys	Girls	Boys	Girls
Childhood nutrition	-0.213***	-0.124***	-0.661***	-0.427***
	(0.053)	(0.043)	(0.229)	(0.145)
Time dummy	0.153	0.157**	0.11	0.166**
	(0.107)	(0.065)	(0.107)	(0.068)
Mother education	0.001	-0.003	0.004	-0.003
	(0.004)	(0.003)	(0.005)	(0.003)
Father education	-0.004	-0.004	-0.005	-0.004
	(0.004)	(0.003)	(0.004)	(0.003)
Age of head of household	0.001	0.000	0.004*	0.001
	(0.002)	(0.001)	(0.002)	(0.001)
# 6-14 yo children in HH	0.024	0.033*	0.031	0.026
	(0.020)	(0.017)	(0.021)	(0.019)
# female adults in HH	0.028	0.031	-0.01	0.034
	(0.029)	(0.021)	(0.029)	(0.023)
# male adults in HH	-0.026	-0.012	-0.032	-0.024
	(0.022)	(0.020)	(0.024)	(0.021)
Per-capita expenditure	-0.011	-0.006	-0.015	-0.033
	(0.027)	(0.022)	(0.029)	(0.020)
Price of rice	-0.112	-0.088	-0.142	-0.149
	(0.100)	(0.095)	(0.106)	(0.092)
Price of sugar	0.105	0.115	0.093	0.114
	(0.128)	(0.118)	(0.129)	(0.126)
Price of cooking oil	0.111*	0.016	0.047	0.034
	(0.066)	(0.047)	(0.068)	(0.046)
Price of condensed milk	-0.173*	-0.151*	-0.137	-0.168*
	(0.103)	(0.085)	(0.103)	(0.087)
Community fixed-effect	Yes	Yes	Yes	Yes
F-stat on the excluded instrument	9.34	19.31	5.77	6.28
(p-value)	(0.000)	(0.000)	(0.000)	(0.000)
Kleibergen-Paap rk LM statistic	45.70	45.98	41.73	32.74
(p-value)	(0.000)	(0.000)	(0.000)	(0.000)
Hansen J stat	5.26	2.30	6.96	1.77
(p-value)	(0.385)	(0.806)	(0.224)	(0.881)
Observations	914	878	914	878

Notes: Dependent variable is whether child experienced delayed primary school enrollment (yes=1). Estimation uses limited information maximum likelihood which is robust to potentially weak instruments. (***), (**), (*) respectively indicate significant at 1, 5 and 10 percent level. Excluded IVs are: interaction rainfall shocks during second and third trimester of *in utero* period and child age (in months), total household assets (log), height of father and mother (cm), age of children (in months) and interaction between number of posyandu in the village and child age, all are in period 1. First-stage regression is in table A3 and A4.

Table 2.7. Heterogeneity impact of childhood nutrition on probability of repeating grade across gender, 2SLS-LIML

Dep. Var: delayed enrollment	Measure of childhood nutrition			
	Height-for age z-score		Non-stunted (Yes=1)	
	Boys	Girls	Boys	Girls
Childhood nutrition	0.011	-0.041	-0.008	0.126
	(0.034)	(0.029)	(0.102)	(0.101)
Time dummy	0.082	0.061	0.087	0.062
	(0.078)	(0.057)	(0.077)	(0.057)
Mother education	-0.006**	-0.003	-0.006**	-0.003
	(0.003)	(0.003)	(0.003)	(0.003)
Father education	-0.001	-0.002	-0.001	-0.002
	(0.003)	(0.002)	(0.003)	(0.002)
Age of head of household	-0.002	0.001	-0.002	0.001
	(0.001)	(0.001)	(0.001)	(0.001)
# 6-14 yo children in HH	0.024	-0.005	0.023	-0.007
	(0.016)	(0.012)	(0.016)	(0.013)
# female adults in HH	0.005	-0.006	0.007	-0.005
	(0.021)	(0.018)	(0.021)	(0.018)
# male adults in HH	0.011	-0.012	0.011	-0.015
	(0.018)	(0.015)	(0.018)	(0.016)
Per-capita expenditure	-0.029*	0.005	-0.029*	-0.004
	(0.017)	(0.018)	(0.017)	(0.016)
Price of rice	-0.001	0.067	-0.003	0.048
	(0.047)	(0.056)	(0.048)	(0.060)
Price of sugar	0.105	-0.094	0.103	-0.096
	(0.121)	(0.099)	(0.120)	(0.102)
Price of cooking oil	-0.078	0.019	-0.074	0.023
	(0.058)	(0.040)	(0.055)	(0.039)
Price of condensed milk	-0.078	0.028	-0.078	0.025
	(0.064)	(0.050)	(0.064)	(0.051)
Community fixed-effect	Yes	Yes	Yes	Yes
F-stat on the excluded instrument	9.34	9.31	5.77	6.28
(p-value)	(0.000)	(0.000)	(0.000)	(0.000)
Kleibergen-Paap rk LM statistic	45.70	45.98	41.73	32.74
(p-value)	(0.000)	(0.000)	(0.000)	(0.000)
Hansen J stat	5.14	0.69	5.18	1.13
(p-value)	(0.399)	(0.984)	(0.394)	(0.951)
Observations	914	878	914	878

Notes: Dependent variable is whether child experienced grade repetition (yes=1). Estimation uses limited information maximum likelihood which is robust to potentially weak instruments. (***), (**), (*) respectively indicate significant at 1, 5 and 10 percent level. Excluded IVs are: interaction rainfall shocks during second and third trimester of *in utero* period and child age (in months), total household assets (log), height of father and mother (cm), age of children (in months) and interaction between number of posyandu in the village and child age, all are in period 1. First-stage regression is in table A3 and A4.

Table 2.8. Impact of midwife exposure on probability of delayed enrollment: 2SLS-LIML

| Dep. Var: delayed enrollment | Measure of childhood nutrition | | | |
| | Height-for age z-score | | Non-stunted (Yes=1) | |
	1	2	3	4
Childhood nutrition	-0.076***	-0.155***	-0.247***	-0.507***
	(0.026)	(0.039)	(0.093)	(0.150)
Childhood Nutrition*Midwife	-0.052	-0.038	-0.188	-0.160
	(0.046)	(0.058)	(0.157)	(0.224)
Midwife	-0.055		0.147	
	(0.062)		(0.051)	
Community fixed-effect	No	Yes	No	Yes
F-test for variables of interest (p-value)				
Childhood nutrition and	15.30	27.67	15.51	24.61
Childhood nutrition*midwife	(0.001)	(0.000)	(0.001)	(0.000)
Midwife and			2.10	
Childhood nutrition*midwife	1.71 (0.425)		(0.349)	
F-stat on the excluded instrument	14.15	10.07	11.73	8.11
(p-value)	(0.000)	(0.000)	(0.000)	(0.000)
Kleibergen-Paap rk LM statistic	135.42	82.43	105.04	62.05
(p-value)	(0.000)	(0.000)	(0.000)	(0.000)
Hansen J stat	8.95	9.90	7.59	8.46
(p-value)	(0.399)	(0.449)	(0.669)	(0.584)
Observations	1910	1890	1910	1890

Notes: Dependent variable is whether child experienced delayed primary school enrollment (yes=1). Other covariates in each specifications (but not displayed here): time dummy, height of parents, age of household head, number of children as well as male and female adults in household, per-capita expenditure, and food prices. Estimation uses limited information maximum likelihood which is robust to potentially weak instruments. (***), (**), (*) respectively indicate significant at 1, 5 and 10 percent level. Excluded IVs in specifications in column 1 & 3 are interaction rainfall shocks during second and third trimester of *in utero* period and child age (in months), total household assets (log), height of father and mother (cm), age of children (in months) and interaction between number of *posyandu* in the village and child age, all are in period 1. For specifications in column 2 and 4 are those as for column 1 and 3 plus their interaction with dummy variable for presence of midwife in period 1. F-test on the excluded instruments for interaction between childhood nutrition and presence of midwife for each specification in column 1,2,3,4 are respectively 6.83, 5.69, 5.26, and 4.46.

Table 2.8A. Partial effect of childhood nutrition on probability of delayed enrollment conditional on the presence of midwife

Proportion of presence of midwife	Height-for-age z-score	Non-stunted (yes=1)
At sample mean (28.7%)	-0.166***	-0.553***
	[0.033]	[0.121]
Simulations:		
Increase presence of midwife to 50%	-0.174***	-0.587***
	(0.033)	(0.118)
Increase presence of midwife to 75%	-0.184***	-0.627***
	(0.039)	(0.138)

Notes: Robust standard errors are in parentheses. Calculations are based on the parameter in table 8 column 2 and 4. (***), (**), (*) respectively indicate significant at 1, 5 and 10 percent level.

Table 2.9. Impact of midwife exposure on probability of repeated grade: 2SLS-LIML

| Dep. Var: delayed enrollment | Measure of childhood nutrition | | | |
| | Height-for age z-score | | Non-stunted (Yes=1) | |
(Yes=1)	1	2	3	4
Childhood nutrition	-0.004	0.02	-0.003	0.138
	(0.022)	(0.029)	(0.075)	(0.108)
Childhood nutrition*Midwife	-0.061*	-0.073*	-0.211*	-0.333**
	(0.037)	(0.043)	(0.127)	(0.162)
Midwife	-0.072		-0.058	
	(0.051)		(0.043)	
Community fixed-effect	No	Yes	No	Yes
F-test for variables of interest (p-value)				
Childhood nutrition and	3.74	2.97	3.65	4.26
Childhood nutrition*midwife	(0.154)	(0.226)	(0.161)	(0.119)
Midwife and			2.98	
Childhood nutrition*midwife	2.91 (0.234)		(0.225)	
F-stat on the excluded instrument	14.15	10.07	11.73	8.11
(p-value)	(0.000)	(0.000)	(0.000)	(0.000)
Kleibergen-Paap rk LM statistic	135.42	82.43	105.04	62.05
(p-value)	(0.000)	(0.000)	(0.000)	(0.000)
Hansen J stat	14.98	13.37	14.29	12.41
(p-value)	(0.133)	(0.185)	(0.162)	(0.259)
Observations	1910	1890	1910	1890

Notes: Dependent variable is whether child experienced grade repetition (yes=1). Other covariates in each specifications (but not displayed here): time dummy, height of parents, age of household head, number of children as well as male and female adults in household, per-capita expenditure, and food prices. Estimation uses limited information maximum likelihood which is robust to potentially weak instruments. (***), (**), (*) respectively indicate significant at 1, 5 and 10 percent level. Excluded IVs in specifications in column 1 & 3 are interaction rainfall shocks during second and third trimester of *in utero* period and child age (in months), total household assets (log), height of father and mother (cm), age of children (in months) and interaction between number of *posyandu* in the village and child age, all are in period 1. For specifications in column 2 and 4 are those as for column 1 and 3 plus their interaction with dummy variable for presence of midwife in period 1. F-test on the excluded instruments for interaction between childhood nutrition and presence of midwife for each specification in column 1,2,3,4 are respectively 6.83, 5.69, 5.26, and 4.46

APPENDICES

Table A2.1. First Stage Regression: Height-for-age z-score

Time dummy	0.395
	(0.165)
Mother education	0.010
	(0.008)
Father education	0.002
	(0.008)
Household head age	-0.002
	(0.004)
# of older children, 6-14 yo	-0.129
	(0.034)
# of adult female	0.114
	(0.054)
# of adult male	-0.053
	(0.044)
PCE (log)	0.233
	(0.048)
price of rice (log)	0.057
	(0.103)
price of sugar (log)	-0.414
	(0.199)
price of cooking oil (log)	0.076
	(0.105)
price of condensed milk (log)	-0.114
	(0.124)
3rd trimester rainfall shock*Age in period 1 (x1000)	-0.033
	(0.011)
2nd trimester rainfall shock*Age in period 1 (x1000)	-0.041
	(0.010)
Assets in period 1 (log)	0.068
	(0.020)
# of posyandu in period 1*age in period 1 (x1000)	-0.025
	(0.065)
Constant	-1.762
	(1.631)

Note: Robust standard errors are in parantheses.

Table A2.2. First Stage Regression: being non-stunted (Yes=1)

Time dummy	0.051
	(0.06)
Mother education	0.006
	(0.00)
Father education	0.001
	(0.00)
Household head age	-0.001
	(0.00)
# of older children, 6-14 yo	-0.035
	(0.01)
# of adult female	0.023
	0.000
# of adult male	-0.02
	(0.014)
PCE (log)	0.06
	(0.016)
price of rice (log)	-0.02
	(0.043)
price of sugar (log)	-0.12
	(0.075)
price of cooking oil (log)	0.04
	(0.034)
price of condensed milk (log)	-0.02
	(0.039)
3rd trimester rainfall shock*Age in period 1 (x1000)	-0.012
	(0.000)
2nd trimester rainfall shock*Age in period 1 (x1000)	-0.01
	(0.000)
Assets in period 1 (log)	0.026
	(0.006)
# of posyandu in period 1*age in period 1 (x1000)	0.003
	(0.000)
Constant	0.62
	(0.56)

Note: Robust standard errors are in parantheses.

CHAPTER 3

AN EVALUATION OF A SUPPLEMENTARY FEEDING PROGRAM IN INDONESIA: IDENTIFICATION USING OF HETEROGENEITY IN PROGRAM EXPOSURE

3.1. Introduction

A growing number of studies have established a link between malnutrition during early childhood and slower physical growth, delayed motor development, lower IQ, and low educational achievement. A related literature has demonstrated an association between improved health and nutritional status during first few years of life with later life outcomes that affect health, education and productivity, including such outcomes as mortality, chronic disease, educational attainment, and returns to labor.[22] In recognition of the consequences of malnutrition, governments in many countries have established programs aiming to reduce or to prevent malnutrition during infancy and early childhood.

A set of public health programs introduced by the Indonesian government and focusing on infant and maternal health fits within this general policy focus found in many developing countries. Basic health programs -- both preventive and curative -- have been delivered to community through village midwives and

---

[22](e.g., Alderman et al 2001; Alderman, Behrman and Hoddinot, 2005; Alderman, Hoddinot and Kinsey 2006; Glewwe, Jacoby and King 2001; Glewwe and King 2001; Maluccio et al 2005; Martorell 1999; and Strauss and Thomas, 1998) .

integrated child health services clinics (*Pos Pelayanan Terpadu*, Posyandu).[23] When

Indonesia was buffeted by economic crisis during 1997 and 1998, the

Government of Indonesia (GOI) launched a supplementary feeding program,

Program Makanan Tambahan (PMT), as part of its broader group of social safety

net programs. The specific aim of the feeding program was to help pregnant

women and children under five years of age cope with adverse effects of the

crisis. The potential importance of the program is evident from the scale of its

rollout from 1998 to 2000.

In this study, we evaluate the effect of a supplementary feeding program

on child health and nutritional status in Indonesia from 1998 to 2000. We

estimate the 'intent-to-treat' effect of the program by quantifying the effect of

program exposure within the community on targeted individuals regardless of

actual participation in the program.[24] The data used for the study come from

two rounds of panel data from Indonesia Family Life Survey (IFLS-2 and IFLS-3)

covering pre- (1997) and post-crisis (2000) periods. The IFLS includes detailed

information on the implementation of Social Safety Net programs, including the

---

[23]The village midwife program was designed to address basic health issues particularly among reproductive age women. Some studies have evaluated the program impact, finding that the placement of a village midwife improved the health of women between 15-49 years old and children between 1-4 years old (see Frankenberg and Thomas, 2001 and Frankenberg, Suriastini and Thomas, 2004). The establishment of Posyandu was aimed, in particular, at maintaining the health and nutritional status of children under 5 year of age through growth monitoring and by providing basic preventive health services and nutritional supplementation.

[24] The use of an *intent-to-treat* approach in evaluating the effect of a program has an important advantage relative to the use of a participation indicator: this approach avoids the complication raised by the fact that participation by individuals is not exogenous.

PMT. The rich household and community panel surveys allow us to contribute to the current literature on program evaluation in two important ways.

First, this is the first study that uses a national panel survey to evaluate the main child nutrition support program implemented by the Indonesia's government during the 1997-98 crisis period. The focus on crisis years should be of interest to researchers as well as policy makers since some studies have shown that there was no significant decline in Indonesian children's health and nutritional status during the crisis period (Block et al, 2005, Frankenberg, Beegle and Thomas, 1999, and Strauss et. al. 2004).[25] A natural question from these findings is whether public programs aiming to support child health and nutritional status helped to prevent declines in health status from occurring.

In addition, using Indonesia for an evaluation of a nutritional program has important short- and long-term policy relevance. While evidence shows an improvement in child health, one indicator of extreme malnutrition, the level of stunting, was comparable in Indonesia in 2000 to many low-income countries in sub-Saharan African. Identifying the effects of the program on child nutritional status promises to provide important guidance as to whether public

---

[25] Strauss et al (2004) provide evidence that lack of change to child health in two IFLS-based studies (Frankenberg et al, 1999 and Strauss et al, 2004) may be due to the fact that survey timing did not coincide with negative shocks to child health. IFLS2+ in 1998 may have occurred too early to detect a negative shock to child health, and IFLS 3 in 2000 may have been too late to capture it. In addition, they note that while there was no strong evidence of a decline in child health during the crisis period, this could also be driven by such factors as drought in the pre-crisis period, or birth or mortality selection.

interventions at a time of crisis may assist in reducing malnutrition among children during and after financial crises.

A second contribution of the paper is methodological. To date, the vast majority of studies in the program evaluation literature make use of a single binary indicator for program exposure. The use of this type of program variable is practical yet may not be able to capture program impact when at least one of two conditions apply: (i) the program is universally distributed, or (ii) the targeted communities receive heterogeneous exposure. The implementation of PMT was characterized by both of these features. In order to evaluate impact in light of this implementation approach, we make use of the detailed information on program implementation available in IFLS-3 and then exploit the heterogeneity in program exposure across communities to estimate the program effect.

Our findings indicate that the program was effective but its impact was limited to children between 12 and 23 months of age. Children from younger and older age groups were not affected by the program. Depending on the specifications used, the program increased the standardized height-for-age of children 12 to 23 months old by 0.48 to 0.55 standard deviations. We also find that the exposure to the program reduced the likelihood of stunting within the same age group by 15 percent by 2000.

This paper is organized as follows. In section 2, we highlight some findings from previous studies on program evaluation, particularly those focusing on Indonesia, and discuss the contribution of this research to the existing literature. Section 3 provides a description about the program and how it was distributed. Section 4 provides an analytical framework, which is then followed by discussions of the data source in section 5. We discuss our empirical strategy and the estimation issues we face in section 6. In Section 7, we present and discuss the results, and provide conclusions in section 8.

3.2. Previous Evaluation Studies on Indonesia Public Health Program

Despite the potential importance of supplementary feeding interventions, there are relatively few efforts to evaluate the effectiveness of these programs in developing countries. In Indonesia, there is only one study evaluating the effectiveness of the post-crisis supplementary feeding program. Sandjaja et al (2001) find little evidence that the program improved nutritional status of targeted children, yet they suggest that the program helped avert a decline of nutritional status among children between 6 and 23 months of age.

The Sandjaja study, however, made use of a small sample size and thus we should be concerned about whether results are generalizable. In addition, the Sandjaja study demonstrated that the program was targeted toward less healthy children, but it fails to address the potential bias to their evaluation from endogenous program placement. In particular, the matching method employed does not control for unobserved heterogeneity likely to be correlated with both the outcome and likelihood of treatment. Moreover, because they were only able to control for post-intervention characteristics of children, the matching

procedure is also likely to select a control group that is not necessarily

comparable with the treated group before the intervention took place. Other

studies have faced similar problems: data are inadequate for evaluation and

often cannot control for program placement.

Other studies evaluating public health programs in Indonesia have

implemented more appropriate strategies to deal with potential bias in

estimating program effects (Frankenberg 1995, Frankenberg and Thomas 2001,

Frankenberg, Suriastini and Thomas 2005, and Gertler and Molyneaux 1994).

With access to more comprehensive and much larger data sets, they control for

endogenous program placement and estimate program effects by implementing

regional fixed-effect or difference-in-difference approaches. Our discussion of

evaluation strategies and results focus on the best of these approaches, found in

the two most recent papers above.[26]

In order to identify effects of placing a midwife within a community,

Frankenberg and Thomas (2001) first compare health status of women in primary

age prior to the introduction of a midwife in a community with the health of the

same individuals after the program. They argue that the program effect may be

contaminated by two sources of unobserved heterogeneity: individual and

community. To deal with unobserved heterogeneity at the individual level, they

---

[26]For additional reviews, see Strauss and Thomas (1995) for review of Frankenberg (1995) and Gertler and Molyneaux (1994).

estimate the effect of a midwife on change in health status. First-differencing

health status eliminates time-invariant forms of individual heterogeneity. They

then include a community fixed-effect to sweep out any time-invariant

unobserved heterogeneity at the community level that may be correlated with

placement of midwives. In addition, they note that the program effect may leak

to some non-targeted groups. To control for such spillovers, they include more

control groups such as primary age males and older males and females in the

regression specification. Their findings indicate that the midwife program

increases body mass index of women in reproductive age by 0.20 more than of

both older and reproductive age men. Their exercise also suggests that the

program has spillover benefits for older women.

Meanwhile, Frankenberg et al (2005) argue that comparing health status of

children residing in a community with a midwife with that of their counterparts

living in a community without a midwife is difficult to interpret due to

confounding impact of the selective assignment of midwives. In order to

measure the midwife effect, they compare the height-for-age of young children

cohort up to 4 years of age, who were exposed to a midwife, with height for age

of older age cohorts who lived in the same community but who were not

exposed to a midwife when young. Their findings show that children who were

fully exposed to a midwife during early childhood had significantly better

height-for-age scores than older children who lived in the same community but

were not exposed to the program.

While the empirical strategy in these two studies may adequately address bias from endogenous program placement, identification rests on a questionable assumption. The use of simple binary program variable implies that the program was implemented homogenously in terms of level and duration across communities. In reality many public health programs are implemented with various types of subprograms or heterogeneous in intensity and exposure (e.g., in terms of duration, supplies, training and additional support). An analysis relying on a simple binary indicator may either overstate or understate the effectiveness of the program.[27]

In sum, only a few studies evaluating public health programs in Indonesia use methodologically sound approaches and data. Other evaluations have relied on limited information regarding program implementation and the distribution of other programs, they often have relied on poor identification strategies, and assumed that programs were distributed with homogenous exposure across regions. Our study addresses these limitations by taking into account the heterogeneity in program exposure and distribution of other similar programs, and, at the same time, controlling for the effects of non-random program placement. We utilize detailed information on implementation and program

---

[27] The use of program intensity as a measure of program exposure was first introduced in the literature by Rosenzweig and Wolpin (1986), but use of such measures have only grown recently (see Dulfo 2001, and more recently Armecin et al 2006, Behrman et al 2004, Gertler 2004, and Yamauchi 2005). Gertler (2004) provides direct comparison of program effects from the two types of program variables, single binary and multiple binary program variables, and shows that both types of program indicators yield significant parameters for program effects. Using multiple dummies for length of program exposure, however, generates more detailed and insightful parameters for characterizing program effects.

features to characterize heterogeneity in program exposure, and then exploit this

heterogeneity to quantify the effect of the supplementary feeding program.

3.3. Analytical Framework

We follow a simple framework introduced by Rosenzweig and Wolpin

(1986) to take into account heterogeneity in program exposure when modeling

the effect of the program on child nutritional status. We assume that preferences

of household members are inter-temporally separable and that in the current

period the household maximizes a quasi-concave utility function over goods,

services and the health status of children:

$$(1) \qquad \max_{X,H} U'(X',H';Z')$$

where X is a vector of consumption goods and services consumed by child i, H is

the health or nutritional status of child i, and Z is a vector of household

characteristics. The production of health (or nutritional status), H, is

characterized by the following production function:

$$(2) \qquad H' = h(N',X',Z',\mu')$$

in which, child health is a function of per child health inputs N, household

characteristics Z, and community characteristics μ –both observed and unobserved. The household also faces a budget constraint in which total

consumption of goods and services as well as health inputs cannot exceed total

income:

$$(3) \qquad Y' = p_x X' + (p_n - s_n) N'$$

where Y is total income, p is price of goods and services X, p, and s respectively

are price and subsidy of health input N.

Solving the optimization problem in equation (1) conditional on equation

(2) and (3) yields a reduced-form health production function for each individual

within the household:

$$(4) \qquad H' = h(p_x, p_n, s'_N, Y', \mu')$$

Our interest here is to identify the impact of public nutrition program on child

nutritional status. Using equation (4) we predict program impact as follows:

$$(5) \qquad \frac{\partial H'}{\partial s'_N} = \frac{\partial H'}{\partial N'} \frac{\partial N'}{\partial s'_N} + \frac{\partial H'}{\partial X'} \frac{\partial X'}{\partial s'_n} + \frac{\partial \mu'}{\partial s'_N}$$

Equation 5 tells that the effect of the program (subsidy) on health or nutritional

status can be decomposed into three components. First is the subsidy effect of

nutritional inputs through the change in demand for nutrition inputs (a price effect). The second component is a change in child nutritional status of program (subsidy) through relocation of resources within household.[28]

The third term is bias which is introduced if the size of the subsidy, s, is affected by unobserved characteristics of children or a community μ. The sign of the bias is ambiguous. It is negative when the government or program distributor follows a compensatory principle, or when a program is distributed more to less-endowed areas, which will thus lead to downward bias in estimates of the true program effect. Conversely, if program is placed more intensively in better endowed areas, the sign of bias becomes positive and the estimated program effect overstates the true effect. Thus unless program s allocation is independent of unobserved heterogeneity μ, an estimation of the program effect must control for these forms of unobserved heterogeneity.

3.4. Nutritional intervention for children during economic crisis.

The goal of supplementary feeding program was to maintain and to improve the nutritional status of children under five, particularly those who were susceptible to the effects of the 1997-98 economic crisis.[29] The program was

---

[28]For example, some research in the literature has found that nutritional intervention programs may be ineffective if parents relocated some nutritional resources away from treated children to other household members.

[29] A monthly supplementary feeding program took place prior to the crisis as part of a public health program. In contrast to post-crisis supplementary feeding program, the pre-crisis program was much less intense and distributed solely through Village Integrated Health Post (*Pos Pelayanan Terpadu, Posyandu*). Under this program, food supplements were delivered along with some basic health services to preschool age children and pregnant women residing in the community.

targeted through a two stage process. First, central and regional governments decided which communities or villages would receive the program. The targeting decision at this stage involved two steps: first, it determined which communities or villages received the program, and second, it decided the length of exposure and intensity of the program in each village. Once a community was assigned to receive the program and program duration was determined, funding was distributed through a public health clinic, *Pusat Kesehatan Masyarakat* (Puskesmas), and a list of children eligible to receive supplementary food was then prepared by the village midwife in consultation with other village leaders, which may have included the village head, women activists, puskesmas staff and family planning field staff.[30]

As with other health programs during 1997/98 economic crisis, program supervision was the responsibility of the village midwife. If a midwife was not available in the community, puskesmas staff assumed responsibility instead.[31] Descriptive information from the IFLS show that in 62 percent of communities, the village midwife administered the program, and in majority of the rest (35 percent of sampled communities), the program was supervised by a member of

---

[30] IFLS data show that although the village midwife was mainly responsible for administering the program, others were also involved in preparing program's recipient list, including the village head or other officials, family planning workers, Puskesmas staff, and community activists.
[31] Village midwives are health workers that are trained to provide basic health services in communities or villages. Their work is coordinated and supervised by the head of *Puskesmas* whose scope of services include one *kecamatan* (an administrative area intermediate in size between the district and the village).

the puskesmas staff.[32] The program was implemented and supplemental food distributed to the community through several different providers. From the IFLS community and facility surveys, we know that the program was implemented by Posyandu in the majority of sampled communities. Other than the Posyandu, village midwifes and village women's association (*Program Kesejahteraan Keluarga*, PKK) also played a role in delivering nutritional supplements to members of the community.[33]

The program targeted poor children between 6 and 59 months of age and pregnant women. The intervention specifically divided targeted children into three sub-groups: (i) infants (6-11 months), (ii) young children (12-23 months), and (iii) children (24-59 months).[34] The majority of communities and villages that received the program during the 1998-2000 period served all of these sub-groups. The community surveys also indicate that in a small portion of communities, non-targeted individuals also received some benefits, including children 5-14 years old, women in reproductive age, the elderly and in some cases, even adult males.

---

[32] The fact that the program was handled by the midwife may raise an issue in identifying the effect of the program. Other health services provided by the midwife might contaminate the estimated the effect of supplementary feeding program. We discuss a strategy to deal with this issue later in empirical section.

[33] Despite the significant role for supplementary food program delivery, some services in *Posyandu* experienced a decline during period 1997-2000. Strauss et al (2004) find that provision of oralit in 2000 decreased by 9.4 percent while child growth monitoring services were 14.1 percent lower relative to 1997.

[34] In addition to children under 5, the program also targeted pregnant women, particularly those women from poor households. Some services provided to this sub-group included pregnancy monitoring and provision of pregnancy vitamins.

Across three sub-groups of children under five years of age, the program differed in terms of quantity, content of diet and the frequency of feedings provided to targeted groups. For infants (6-11 months), supplemental diets were provided in the form of soft meals to supplement breast milk. The nutritional composition per 100 grams of food included 360-430 kcal of energy and 10-15 grams of protein, and this was provided 3 to 4 times a day for 180 consecutive days. Young children (12-23 months) and children between 24-59 months received a locally prepared snack with a nutritional composition that included energy (360-430 kcal) and protein (9-11 grams) for 90 consecutive days. The difference in the program between the two older groups was that for younger children, a snack was provided three to four times a day, and for older children it was only provided once a week.

The program was introduced in early 1998 but not all communities received it at the same time. The program coverage, as indicated in Table 1, was low at the beginning of the crisis (the end of 1997 and early 1998) because the crisis was not anticipated in the 1997-1998 fiscal budget.[35] It was only during the following fiscal year (1998-1999) that coverage of the program expanded above 70 percent, and then further expanded to over 90 percent in 1999-2000, before it

---

[35] The national budget plan (fiscal year) in Indonesia prior to year of 2001 ran from April 1 to March 31. After 2001, the government of Indonesia adjusted change the fiscal year to correspond to the calendar year.

declined to 82 percent during the first half of fiscal year 2000-2001.[36] Overall,

during the 1998-2000 period, most of the sampled communities (94.7 percent)

were exposed to the program.

3.5. Data and variables measurement

The data used in this study come from two rounds (1997 and 2000) of

Indonesia Family Life Survey (IFLS), which covers periods before and after the

1997-1998 Asian Financial Crisis and implementation of child supplementary

food program. The IFLS is a panel survey that collects data on various aspects of

individual, household and family livelihood. The survey also collects

information about facilities and conditions in the communities where households

and individuals reside, including important characteristics of the socio-economic

environment, physical infrastructure, and health and education facilities.[37] In this

study we link community-level data on implementation of the supplementary

feeding program since the beginning of the crisis in 1998 with individual-level

data on health and nutritional status of children.

Our sample for this study includes all children who were between 6 and

59 months in 1997 and 2000, and lived in IFLS sampled communities (2170 and

2618, respectively). The average age of these children in 1997 and 2000 was 34.12

---

[36] Pritchett et al (2002) mention that the initial fiscal year 1998-1999 did not include a post for emergency programs to broadly cope with negative impact of crisis. It was only July 1998 that the ongoing budget was revised and thus contained an item for Social Safety Net Program.
[37] Sampling and survey methods for IFLS2 and IFLS3 can be found in Frankenberg, Beegle and Thomas (1999) and Strauss et al (2004b), respectively.

and 32.67 months, respectively. Information from the community and facility survey of the IFLS indicates that fewer than 4 percent of the sampled communities provided program benefits to non-targeted groups (non-pregnant women, children 5-14 years old and other adults). For this reason, we believe that the proportion of non-targeted children who were exposed to the program is negligible.

We use child standardized height-for-age as our measure of nutritional status. The health literature suggests that, in terms of measurement error, this is a less problematic indicator for child health and nutritional status than other alternative health measures.[38] The use of a standardized height-for-age measure to represent health and nutritional status outcomes is appropriate as we believe that the impact of crisis, if any, should be evident using a measure that captures longer-term impacts.

In order to focus on more extreme effects, we also examine the proportion of children who suffer from stunting, or who have standardized height-for-age measures of less than negative 2. This measure represents deficit in standardized height-for-age (less than or equal to -2) and often refers in medical literature as *shortness*. We calculate standardized height-for-age using a STATA ado program called *zanthro* (Vidmar et al, 2004). In *zanthro*, standardized height-for-age are calculated by comparing the actual child height in the IFLS sample with those

---

[38] In IFLS, height and weight are measured by trained health workers with regularly calibrated health equipment. We believe that enumeration protocols helped to limit measurement error for this variable.

from a US reference population found in the 2000 Center for Disease Control and Prevention (CDC) Growth Charts.

In Table 2, we show the mean child standardized of height-for-age and proportion of stunting in 1997 and 2000 and change in these statistics over the two survey rounds. We observe a positive but insignificant change in child standardized height-for-age from 1997 to 2000 among children between 6 and 59 months of age. A stronger improvement in nutritional status was found in a significant reduction in stunting.[39] The reduction in stunting, however, is only significant for the older groups (12-23 months and 24-59 months). Specifically, the proportion of 12-23 months and 24-59 months children who were stunted decreased by 8.3 and 2.8 percent, respectively, from 1997 to 2000. We found no change in the stunted share of children from 6-11 months of age. This descriptive underscores findings documented by Strauss et al (2004), which suggested that nutritional status of children 6-59 months of age did not deteriorate during the crisis period.

As discussed above, a simple binary program variable to measure program impact may be inadequate for two reasons. First, as shown in Table 1, the program was found in majority of communities, and use of a program dummy (with 1 indicating access to the program, and 0 otherwise) may not

---

[39]A child exhibits stunting if his or her standardized height for age is less than or equal to negative two.

guarantee sufficient variation between those with access to the program and those who lack it.

In addition, the use of a binary program exposure variable in an evaluation exercise implicitly assumes that program was implemented with homogenous exposure on its targeted subjects within and across communities. If a program was implemented with different exposure across communities, the use of a binary program exposure dummy may lead us to underestimate the program impact. Sandjaja et al (2001) and the IFLS community surveys document differences in content, quality and duration of the program across communities.

To better identify program impact, we also use an alternative measure better suited to capturing heterogeneity in program exposure across targeted individuals. Specifically, we use proportion of life in which a child was exposed to the program. The measure is generated by combining the age of children who lived in the treatment villages and length of time that the program existed in the community. The program length is generated by using information on the start and end dates of the program in each community. [40],[41]

---

[40] In IFLS3, community informant was asked about details of program implementation, including the beginning and the ending date of the program, the kinds of food given to the recipients, the program administrator, and other information.

[41] One might use program length itself as other alternative measure. However there are two issues when estimating program effect using this measure. First, it assigns the same length of exposure value to each child living in the community regardless of age. Thus, this measure fails to pick up variation in program exposure among targeted children living within similar community. Second, program length is very likely to be endogenous as the government might systematically distribute or phase in the program based on some criteria that were not observed by program evaluator.

We follow an approach first introduced by Rosenzweig and Wolpin (1986) to combine information on variation in child age and the timing of program introduction to construct an index measure of program exposure. In particular, let (t_s, t_p, t_b) represent date of the survey, date in which the program is first introduced in community v, and birth date of a child, respectively. We assume that the program will have different exposure across children depending on the age of children and the duration of the program in the community. For example, a child born before the introduction of the program will be exposed for t_s-t_p years. Letting PMT_{iv}^a represent program exposure of child i in community v who was age a at the survey date, where $a=t_s$-t_b, we calculate the program exposure variable as:

PMT_{iv}^a =0 if the program does not exist in the community v when the survey was held,

$$= ((t_s - t_p)/a) \text{ if } t_s \geq t_p \geq t_b \text{ in community } v,$$

$$= 1 \text{ if } t_s \geq t_b \geq t_p \text{ in community } v.$$

This variable thus measures the proportion of a child's life with exposure to the program and varies between 0 and 1 and this varies across children. "1" indicates that a child has been exposed for his or her entire life, or 100 percent exposure. This occurs when a child was born after the introduction of the program and when the program was still active at the time of the last survey

(2000). Therefore, only children who were born in 1998 or afterward, or those who were between 6 to 35 months old, could have full program exposure. In contrast, "0" indicates that a child was not exposed at all to the program. This value is assigned to children who lived in a community without the program in 1997 and 2000 or those who lived in community without the program but were 5 years old or older in 1998. Values between 0 and 1 reflect children who were exposed for some part of their life, but were born at least six months before the introduction the program. Table 3 shows mean program exposure for each of the targeted groups which are also disaggregated into various sub-groups for the 2000 sample.

We also control for other covariates to isolate the effect of the program on child nutritional status. These covariates cover biological, socio-economic and demographic characteristics that are likely to be correlated with child nutritional status. Other than child age and gender, we control for mother's height and education, and per capita expenditure as well as additional community characteristics (see Table 4 for a list of community characteristics). Table 4 shows descriptive statistics for important household and community level characteristics.

3.6. Empirical Identification and Specification

We start with standard econometric specification to estimate the effect of supplementary feeding program on child nutritional status:

$$H_{ivt} = \alpha_0 + \alpha_1 T_t + \alpha_2 PMT_v^a + \beta PMT_v^a * T_t + \varepsilon_{ivt} \qquad (6)$$

where H is the health outcome variable which is the nutritional status (using anthropometric measures) of child i living in community v at time t, T is dummy variable for time period, and PMT is a program exposure variable (which may be binary or continuous in alternative specifications).

Our parameter of interest in equation 6, β, is a difference-in-difference estimator which measures the impact of the program on the treatment group. When using a binary program variable, the treatment group is comprised of the communities and villages that received the program. The control group is all children residing in a village or community without the program. Therefore β measures change of nutritional status among children under 5 who lived in treatment villages relative to those who lived in control villages. Because nearly all communities were exposed to the program for some amount of time after 1998 and none of communities in 1997 received it, β essentially compares nutritional status of children in 2000 relative to 1997.

Other parameters in (6) are also of potential interest. α_1 measures any common change in child nutritional status that is not associated with the program. One of the effects captured by α_1 will be the effect of the crisis, which we expect to be negative. Meanwhile α_2 will pick up features of communities that may affect nutritional status independent of the program itself.

The estimated program effect from (6), however, is likely to be biased. Program allocation may be correlated with omitted characteristics of communities receiving the program. Even worse, many of these omitted variables are unobserved by the analyst. To deal with this issue, one approach is to control for unobserved heterogeneity by including community fixed-effect. This procedure implicitly assumes that unobserved factors that are correlated with the program are all at the community level and are time-invariant. In addition we include household characteristics, Z^h, and time-varying community characteristics, Z^v, to increase the efficiency of the parameter of interest. Including community fixed-effect and some community and household-level covariates, suggests the following model:

$$H_{ivt} = \alpha_0 + \alpha_1 T_t + \beta PMT_v^a * T_t + \delta_1 Z_{ivt}^h + \delta_2 Z_{vt}^c + \mu_v + \varepsilon_{ivt} \qquad (7)$$

Controlling for a community fixed-effect in this model, will control for *PMT* placement and other time-invariant community characteristics. We control for placement through the fixed effect, and then focus our attention on β, our main parameter of interest.

The use of binary program variable in our case may not accurately capture program effect. This is because the program, as previously shown, was heterogeneously exposed to the communities. Simplifying and treating it as it was homogenously distributed across communities implies that all targeted children lived in the communities with program would be fully exposed to the program irrespective the length of program has been in the community and the age of children. The estimated parameter of interest when using binary program variable provides an upper bound program effect.

We then propose an alternative measure of program variable. Information on the starting and ending dates of the program together with child's birth place and birth date are used to calculate the proportion of child age exposed to the program and to identify how exposure to the program affects nutritional status of children. We expect, ceteris paribus, that the higher the proportion of child's age exposed to the program, the greater the improvement in nutritional status and the less likely that targeted children showed stunting in 2000.

The estimation procedure when using proportion of child's age that is exposed to the program as program variable should principally be similar with the estimation using binary program variable. The only difference is that the program variable is no longer a simple binary program indicator, but instead ranges from 0 to 1. In addition, this alternative program variable has the benefit of varying by child rather than community. This alternative program variable provides us with a strategy for identifying program effects while also controlling for community-level unobserved heterogeneity.

After controlling for (potential) endogenous program placement, a time dummy (to control for common change in program outcome across periods), Z^h and Z^c, our identifying assumption in estimating the program effect is that unobserved factors captured in the error term ε are uncorrelated with our program effect variable. Given that assumption holds, β thus indicates the effectiveness of the program. Prior to estimating equation 7, we also investigate what factors affect allocation of program and program intensity across communities. To do so, we estimate determinants of program duration at the community level.

3.7. Results and Analysis

3.7.1. Determinants of Program Duration

As noted above, the program was found in almost all communities during the period from 1998 to 2000, but we observe variation in program length across communities. In this section, we ask what factors, if any, affect variation in program exposure across communities. We estimate the program length on all 1997 covariates, including health status, socio-economic status, health and physical infrastructure as well as some variables that proxy remoteness of the community using pooled OLS. We also include district fixed-effect to control for district-level unobserved heterogeneity that may have affected timing of program implementation.

Estimation results are shown in Table 5. Without measures of community nutritional status in the specification (model 1 of table 5), three variables associated with remoteness of the community appear to be statistically different from zero. In addition, joint significance tests on the group of variables associated with remoteness confirm the importance of these factors for allocation of the program. The signs on coefficients of two variables, distance from district capital and availability of public transportation, imply that more remote communities were exposed to the program for a longer period of time. The coefficient on another indicator, whether the community is urban, indicates that the urban community tends to receive longer program exposure relative to rural communities between 1998 and 2000.

If program allocation during 1998-2000 was based entirely on 1997 characteristics as modeled here, the finding that urban communities received longer treatment would be inconsistent with the fact that nutritional status in urban communities in 1997 was better than in rural areas (see figure 3.1 and 3.2). However the allocation procedure might also be based on the community characteristics in 1998 and 1999, or changes from 1997, which we cannot observe in the IFLS.

We then include two different measures of nutritional status in model 2 and 3, one is 1997 average height-for-age of children under 5 and the other is proportion of children living in the community in 1997 who were stunted. Our three measure of remoteness have consistent signs and significance when we include community average indicators of child health. The coefficient on 1997 average height-for-age has a negative sign, which implies that communities with healthier children tended to receive the program for a shorter amount of time than communities where average nutritional status was worse, but the coefficient is not significantly different from zero. When using the share of children who were stunted in the community, however, we find a strong and significant predictor of program duration.

Descriptive evidence shown in Figures 3.1, 3.2, 3.3 and 3.4 provides additional information on how program was distributed. Figure 3.1 plots the average height-for-age distribution for urban and rural communities in 1997. It shows that over most of the distribution, average child height-for-age is greater in urban communities. There appear to be crossing points of the two curves in the lower and upper tail when average height-for-age z-scores are -2.2 and -0.2, respectively, and this indicates that in the lower tail average health status may be worse for some urban communities. Figure 3.2 enlarges the lower tail of figure 3.1 and it shows, consistent with figure 3.1, that proportion of stunted children was higher in rural communities than urban ones except for upper part of the distribution. Using per capita expenditure, we also find that urban households have a higher per capita expenditure in 1997 than rural households (Figure 3.4).

Given these distributions of child nutritional status measures and per capita expenditure in 1997, one might expect that rural communities would be exposed to the program for a longer period. But figure 3.4, supports our finding in table 5, and shows that up to the 20 month point, urban communities were exposed to the program for more time during the 1998-2000 period. The exception is probably in the upper part of distribution, to the right side of the crossing point at 20 months, where the distribution of program length was essentially equal. These findings imply that the program might be properly distributed only to communities with severe malnutrition problems. In communities with less severe nutritional problems, the program seemed to be biased toward urban rather than rural communities.

The observable characteristics may not include enough information to conclude that the program was properly targeted. There may be other information that cannot be observed and controlled for with our data here that explain why program length distribution tended to be urban biased. For example, Frankenberg et al (1999) use data that capture changes in people's well-being at the beginning of the crisis and find that urban communities experienced larger increases in the proportion of households living below the poverty line.[42] Yet they also find that during 1997-1998, there was little evidence showing that child health and nutritional status had deteriorated significantly, and this is consistent with evidence cited by Block et al (2004) and Strauss et al (2004). They do not show how changes in child health and nutritional status vary between urban and rural communities.

3.7.2. The effect of supplementary feeding program.

In order to control for the different benefits and protocols across the three targeted age groups, we perform our analyses separately for children who are 6-11 months, 12-23 months and 24-59 months. Table 6 presents estimation results

---

[42] Frankenberg et al (1999) use IFLS2 and IFLS2+ which cover the period before and the beginning of the crisis –up to November 1998.

for the effect of the program on child nutritional status using a binary indicator for presence of the program in 1998 and 2000.[43] We first present pooled OLS and then include community fixed-effect models to control for unobserved community characteristics systematically related to program implementation. The results shown in Table 6 suggest that the sign for estimated effects of the program on child standardized height-for-age, except for infant 6-11 months, are negative, but not statistically significant. The inclusion of community fixed-effect, not community characteristics, largely increases the coefficient of program effect as well as R-squared and therefore F-test score, but the program effect remains statistically insignificant. With almost all sampled communities receiving the program during 1998-2000, and very little variation in program exposure, it is not surprising that we find an insignificant program effect. In addition, the coefficient on the year dummy is negative, an indication of how the 1997/98 economic crisis may have affected child nutritional status, but the effect is statistically insignificant.

Next, we estimate models examining program impact on probability of stunting (height-for-age is less than or equals to -2) in 2000 using the binary program variable. The signs on the parameter of interest are consistent with initial expectation except for the group of children 24-59 months. The program only appeared to be effective in lowering the probability of stunting in 2000

---

[43]Table 6 presents a summary of results, the full set of parameter estimates are shown in Appendix Tables A7.2.1 and A7.2.3.

among infant 6-11 months when we control for unobserved heterogeneity using with community fixed effects. In particular, community fixed-effect estimates (model 3 of Table 7) indicate that exposure to the program reduced the probability of stunting in 2000 by 33 percent. Meanwhile when the community fixed-effect estimates include time-varying community characteristics in the specification, the exposure to the program lowers the probability of being stunted in 2000 by 39 percent. However this estimated effect is likely to overestimate the true effect since binary program variable when program exists ($PMT=1$) implies a full exposure to the program for all targeted children living in the community with the program.

We next use fraction of child age exposed to the program to capture heterogeneity in program exposure to identify the program effect. We argue that this program variable measures program effect more accurately as this measure takes into account the heterogeneity of program exposure across communities and variation in potential exposure among targeted children. Results of estimated effects on height for age are shown in Table 8, and the full estimation results are presented in Tables A3.7.2.7 and A3.7.2.9. Estimation using pooled OLS (with and without time-varying community characteristics in the specifications) yields parameters of interest with mixed signs, but all are statistically insignificant (model 1 and 2 of table 8). When including community fixed-effects, our estimation produces positive and significant program effects on height-for-age of children 12-23 months of age (panel B of table 8). In particular, our results suggest that exposure to the program increased child standardized height-for-age between 0.48 and 0.55 standard deviations, depending on whether or not time-varying community characteristics are included. The estimated effects are statistically significant at the 5 percent level. The estimated effect of the program on children 24-59 months is negative and statistically insignificant, which is also what we found when using the binary program indicator. Our findings for infants between 6 and 11 months are negative and insignificant when including community fixed-effects and this is inconsistent with findings using the binary program variable. These findings, however, make sense since estimation using binary program variable is very likely to overestimate the program effect since it implicitly assumes that all targeted individuals were fully exposed during all their life span in the exposed communities.

We next use exposure to the program to evaluate the effectiveness of the program on reducing the probability of children being stunted in 2000 relative to 1997. We find that the program helped children with severe malnutrition problems during the 1997-2000 period, but only the children in 12 to 23 month age group. In particular, exposure to the program reduced the probability of being stunted in 2000 by about 15 percent, and this effect is statistically significant at the 10 percent level. Unlike in previous estimations, the inclusion of community characteristicsconly had a slight impact on the magnitude of the effect. On the other hand, we also found that the program did not reduce stunting in children in the 6-11 month and 24-59 month age groups.

We draw additional comfort in our results because other parameter estimates, such as coefficients on child age and parent's human capital (education and health), are consistent with findings elsewhere in the economics literature (tables A3.7.2.1-A3.7.2.12). In particular, age (in months) exhibits a non-linear relationship with health and nutritional status of children. There is a negative relationship only until children reach 24 months and then this relationship is positive as children age beyond 24 months. Education of parents, particularly mother's education, is also important for improving nutritional status of children, but only for older children (24-59 months). Although we see a positive association between father's education and the nutritional status of children, the relationship is not statistically different from zero. On the other hand, parent's height (in cm), which proxies for parent well-being when in early childhood and cognitive capacity, is positively associated with child nutritional status. The effect is strong across models and specifications regardless type of program variable used in the model.

3.8. Summary and Conclusions

This paper evaluates the effectiveness of a supplementary feeding program for maintaining child nutritional status through the period of the 1997-1998 economic crises in Indonesia. Since the program was nearly universal in its implementation, use of a simple binary indicator to measure program exposure may not allow us to accurately capture the program effect. With access to

86

detailed information on program implementation, we exploit heterogeneity in program exposure to evaluate the program effect.

The use of program heterogeneity has at least two advantages for identifying the effect of Indonesia's supplemental feeding program. First use of program exposure allows us to estimate an effect even with low variation of program distribution across targeted subjects. Second, use of the program allows us to avoid the strong assumption that all targeted children experienced homogenous exposure to the program and therefore allows us to capture the program effect more accurately than when using a binary program indicator.

We show that although the program tended to be universally distributed during 1998-2000, the distribution of program length varied across communities. We also provide insight into the government's implicit allocation rule when determining program length. Community-level average child health outcomes are important factors influencing duration of exposure to the problem.

Findings on the effect of program exposure show that the program improved the nutritional status of children 12 to 23 months of age during the period of economic crisis, and in particular, improved standardized height-for-age by an average of 0.48 to 0.55 standard deviations. Given the increase of standardized height-for-age for all sampled children between 1997 and 2000 was only 0.04, this implies that the crisis would have otherwise led to a negative impact on child nutritional status if the program was not launched. Our findings also suggest that the program helped children with severe malnutrition problems, but again the impact was limited to those who were 12-23 months.

Putting this finding together with results from targeting regression suggests that program could have been more effective and had significant impact on broader targeted groups if it was targeted more properly to communities with worse health problem. Since we know, for example, that the nutritional status of rural children was on average lower than their urban counterparts in 1997, the program would have probably had more impact if it was allocated more to rural communities.

Our results also highlight the potential benefit of using heterogeneity in program exposure when evaluating a universally targeted program. The use of program intensity is not just helpful to capture program effects as it can also be used to in conjunction with community fixed effects in a way that avoids bias from endogenous program placement. Such benefits suggest that future surveys continue to collect information on program implementation.

Table 3.1. Distribution of PMT Coverage Across Communities, 1998-2000

	Total	Urban	Rural
Communities with PMT from 1998-2000 (%)	94.68	56.48	38.21
In the 1998/1999 fiscal year (%)	71.10	43.52	27.57
In the 1999/2000 fiscal year (%)	92.69	56.81	35.88
In the 2000/2001 fiscal year* (%)	82.72	49.17	33.55

Note: Number of communities in the sample is 301. (*) indicates the fiscal year ended in December.

Table 3.2. Standardized Height-for-Age and Incidence of Stunting:
Children between 6 and 59 months in 1997 & 2000

	1997	2000	Diff
6-11 Months			
Mean	-0.96	-0.90	0.06
	(0.12)	(0.07)	(0.13)
Stunted (%)	20.29	16.67	-3.62
	(0.03)	(0.02)	(0.03)
Observations	207	318	
12-23 Months			
Mean	-1.66	-1.62	0.04
	(0.06)	(0.05)	(0.08)
Stunted (%)	36.32	28.05	-8.28**
	(0.02)	(0.02)	(0.03)
Observations	468	574	
24-59 months			
Mean	-1.60	-1.56	0.04
	(0.03)	(0.03)	(0.04)
Stunted (%)	35.12	32.33	-2.79*
	(0.01)	(0.01)	(0.02)
Observations	1495	1726	

Notes: Calculated from IFLS data. Standard errors are in parentheses. (*) is
significant at 10%; (**) is significant at 5%; (***) is significant at 1%.

Table 3.3. Mean Child Exposure to Supplementary Feeding Program, Children 6-59 Months in 2000.

	All groups	Gender		Community	
		Boy	Girl	Urban	Rural
6-11 months	0.34	0.34	0.33	0.36	0.32
Observations	4788	271	254	230	295
12-23 months	0.26	0.27	0.24	0.30	0.23
Observations	1576	526	516	474	568
24-59 months	0.14	0.14	0.14	0.14	0.14
Observations	3221	1625	1596	1364	1857

Notes: Calculated from IFLS3 data.

Table 3.4. Descriptive Statistics

Variable	Mean	Std. Dev.
Mother's education	6.38	6.15
Father's education	6.65	4.13
Mother's height	150.27	5.13
Father's height	160.77	6.24
Gender of HH head (male=1)	0.88	0.32
Main activity of HH (farm=1)	0.40	0.49
HH access to private toilet (Yes=1)	0.57	0.49
HH access to sanitation (Yes=1)	0.19	0.39
Per-capita expenditure ('000s RP)	215.2	728.3
Type of community (urban=1), C	0.43	0.50
Distance of comm. to bus station (km), C	4.23	7.09
Prop. of land with technical irigation, C	0.08	0.18
Asphalt road in the comm (Yes=1), C	0.76	0.43
Village has sewerage (Yes=1), C	0.54	0.50
Village has piped water (Yes=1), C	0.56	0.50

Notes: Calculated from IFLS3 data (C), Indicates Community-Level Variables

Table 3.5. Determinants of Program Length across Communities 1997-2000 (pooled OLS)

Model	(1)	(2)	(4)
Health Status			
Average Height-for-Age	-	-0.87	-
		(0.90)	
Proportion of Children Stunted (%)	-	-	4.61*
			(2.64)
Sociol-economic status			
Average Per-Capita Expenditure	-0.91	-0.7	-0.47
	(1.16)	(1.19)	(1.20)
Farm Household Share (%)	-3.01	-2.72	-2.73
	(2.77)	(2.80)	(2.76)
Share of Households with Male Head (%)	1.43	1.28	1.35
	(2.12)	(2.10)	(2.10)
Physical Infrastructure			
Availability of Asphalt Road (Yes=1)	2.1	2.02	2.07
	(1.77)	(1.76)	(1.76)
Proportion of Land with Semi-Tech Irrigation (%)	-4.25	-4.18	-4.7
	(4.02)	(3.96)	(3.88)
Access to piped water (yes=1)	0.12	0.15	0.15
	(1.39)	(1.38)	(1.38)
Remoteness of community			
Distance to District Capital (km)	0.04*	0.04*	0.04*
	(0.02)	(0.02)	(0.02)
Distance to Bus Station (km)	-0.14	-0.14	-0.15
	(0.10)	(0.10)	(0.10)
Public Transportation in Community (Yes=1)	-4.30***	-4.30***	-4.39***
	(1.53)	(1.52)	(1.52)
Urban Community (Yes=1)	2.61*	2.75*	2.78*
	(1.56)	(1.56)	(1.55)
District Fixed-Effect	Yes	Yes	Yes
R-squared	0.24	0.25	0.25
F-test (economic status) (p-value)	0.79	0.59	0.53
	(0.50)	(0.62)	(0.66)
F-test (infrastructure) (p-value)	0.80	0.78	0.90
	(0.49)	(0.51)	(0.44)
F-test (remoteness of community) (p-value)	3.18	3.18	3.26
	(0.01)	(0.01)	(0.01)

Notes: Dependent variable is number of months the program was in the community between 1998-2000. Independent variables are community averages of 1997 covariates. Standard errors are in parentheses. (*), (**) and (***) indicate significance respectively at 10%, 5% and 1%.

Table 3.6. The Effect of PMT on Height-for-Age of Children 6-59 Months: Binary Program Indicator

	Pooled OLS		Community Fixed-Effects	
	(1)	(2)	(3)	(4)
A. 6-11 Months				
Year Dummy (2000=1)	-0.22	-0.301	-0.41	-0.516
	(0.395)	(0.397)	(0.702)	(0.707)
Program Since '98 (Yes=1)*Year	0.248	0.365	0.51	0.62
	(0.384)	(0.387)	(0.711)	(0.723)
Community Characteristics Included	No	Yes	No	Yes
R-squared	0.14	0.16	0.57	0.58
B. 12-23 Months				
Year Dummy (2000=1)	0.027	-0.02	0.09	0.099
	(0.230)	(0.234)	(0.239)	(0.256)
Program Since '98 (Yes=1)*Year	-0.108	-0.052	-0.073	-0.06
	(0.225)	(0.230)	(0.265)	(0.280)
Community Characteristics Included	No	Yes	No	Yes
R-squared	0.08	0.08	0.40	0.40
B. 24-59 months				
Year Dummy (2000=1)	0.074	0.102	0.114	0.126
	(0.136)	(0.137)	(0.186)	(0.186)
Program Since '98 (Yes=1)*Year	-0.135	-0.157	-0.138	-0.153
	(0.133)	(0.134)	(0.190)	(0.191)
Community Characteristics Included	No	Yes	No	Yes
R-squared	0.15	0.15	0.27	0.27

Note: The dependent variable is the child height for age z-score, and the program effect is a dummy for whether the community had a supplemental feeding program interacted with a dummy for year=2000. Covariates include (but not reported in this table) mother education and height, male head of household, farm household, per capita expenditure, household access to private toilet, sanitation and free health services, distance of village to bus station, community's access to sewerage and piped water, number of village midwife and *posyandu* in the community, and type of community. Robust standard errors are in parentheses. (*), (**) and (***) indicate significance respectively at 10%, 5% and 1%.

Table 3.7. The Effect of PMT on Probability of Stunting Among Children 6-59 of Age: Binary Program Indicator

	Pooled OLS		Community Fixed-effects	
	(1)	(2)	(3)	(4)
A. 6-11 Months				
Year Dummy (2000=1)	0.07	0.085	0.223	0.277
	(0.107)	(0.108)	(0.199)	(0.204)
Program Since '98 (Yes=1)*Year	-0.124	-0.144	-0.332	-0.399
	(0.104)	(0.105)	(0.196)*	(0.202)**
Community Characteristics	No	Yes	No	Yes
R-squared	0.10	0.11	0.53	0.54
B. 12-23 Months				
Year Dummy (2000=1)	-0.076	-0.058	0.02	0.044
	(0.087)	(0.088)	(0.149)	(0.152)
Program Since '98 (Yes=1)*Year	0.019	-0.007	-0.099	-0.123
	(0.085)	(0.087)	(0.154)	(0.158)
Community Characteristics	No	Yes	No	Yes
R-Squared	0.08	0.09	0.38	0.38
B. 24-59 Months				
Year Dummy (2000=1)	-0.008	-0.014	-0.037	-0.039
	(0.053)	(0.054)	(0.071)	(0.071)
Program Since '98 (Yes=1)*Year	0.013	0.019	0.045	0.049
	(0.052)	(0.053)	(0.072)	(0.072)
Community Characteristics	No	Yes	No	Yes
R-squared	0.11	0.12	0.22	0.22

Note: There are 4788 observations. The dependent is an indicator for whether the child has a height for age z score less than -2, and the program effect is a dummy for whether the community had a supplemental feeding program interacted with a dummy for year=2000. Covariates include (but not reported in this table) mother education and height, male head of household, farm household, per capita expenditure, household access to private toilet, sanitation and free health services, distance of village to bus station, community's access to sewerage and piped water, number of village midwife and *posyandu* in the community, and type of community. Robust standard errors are in parentheses. (*), (**) and (***) indicate significance respectively at 10%, 5% and 1%.

Table 3.8. The Effect of PMT on Height-for-Age of Children 6-59 Months: Proportion of Age Exposed to the Program

	Pooled OLS		Community Fixed-Effects	
	(1)	(2)	(3)	(4)
A. 6-11 Months				
Year Dummy (2000=1)	0.044	0.118	-0.036	-0.052
	(0.172)	(0.173)	(0.343)	(0.358)
Age Exposed to the Program*Year	-0.048	-0.128	0.219	0.24
	(0.187)	(0.190)	(0.477)	(0.501)
Community Characteristics	No	Yes	No	Yes
R-Squared	0.14	0.16	0.57	0.58
B. 12-23 Months				
Year Dummy (2000=1)	-0.093	-0.089	-0.213	-0.227
	(0.104)	(0.105)	(0.145)	(0.152)
Age Exposed to the Program *Year	0.035	0.04	0.482	0.552
	(0.125)	(0.126)	(0.229)**	(0.237)**
Community Characteristics	No	Yes	No	Yes
R-Squared	0.08	0.09	0.41	0.41
B. 24-59 Months				
Year Dummy (2000=1)	-0.023	-0.009	0.009	0.002
	(0.058)	(0.058)	(0.071)	(0.073)
Age Exposed to the Program *Year	-0.12	-0.143	-0.095	-0.072
	(0.117)	(0.118)	(0.171)	(0.174)
Community Characteristics	No	Yes	No	Yes
R-Squared	0.15	0.15	0.27	0.27

Note: Dependent variable is child height for age z-score. Covariates include (but not reported in this table) mother education and height, male head of household, farm household, per capita expenditure, household access to private toilet, sanitation and free health services, distance of village to bus station, community's access to sewerage and piped water, number of village midwife and *posyandu* in the community, and type of community. Robust standard errors are in parentheses. (*), (**) and (***) indicate significance respectively at 10%, 5% and 1%.

Table 3.9. The Effect of PMT on the Probability of Stunting Among Children 6-59 Months: Proportion of Age Exposed to the Program

	Pooled OLS		Community Fixed-Effects	
	(1)	(2)	(3)	(4)
A. 6-11 Months				
Year Dummy (2000=1)	-0.052	-0.06	-0.064	-0.061
	(0.047)	(0.047)	(0.100)	(0.103)
Age Exposed to the Program *Year	0.006	0.012	-0.061	-0.08
	(0.051)	(0.052)	(0.130)	(0.134)
Community Characteristics	No	Yes	No	Yes
R-Squared	0.09	0.11	0.52	0.53
B. 12-23 Months				
Year Dummy (2000=1)	-0.072	-0.079	0.003	0.006
	(0.039)*	(0.040)**	(0.053)	(0.056)
Age Exposed to the Program *Year	0.028	0.028	-0.154	-0.155
	(0.047)	(0.048)	(0.082)*	(0.084)*
Community Characteristics	No	Yes	No	Yes
R-squared	0.08	0.09	0.38	0.38
B. 24-59 Months				
Year Dummy (2000=1)	-0.009	-0.01	-0.014	-0.01
	(0.023)	(0.023)	(0.027)	(0.028)
Age Exposed to the Program *Year	0.049	0.053	0.075	0.062
	(0.046)	(0.046)	(0.068)	(0.069)
Community Characteristics	No	Yes	No	Yes
R-Squared	0.11	0.12	0.22	0.22

Note: There are 4788 observations. The dependent is an indicator for whether the child has a height for age z score less than -2. Covariates include (but not reported in this table) mother education and height, male head of household, farm household, per capita expenditure, household access to private toilet, sanitation and free health services, distance of village to bus station, community's access to sewerage and piped water, number of village midwife and *posyandu* in the community, and type of community. Robust standard errors are in parentheses. (*), (**) and (***) indicate significance respectively at 10%, 5% and 1%.

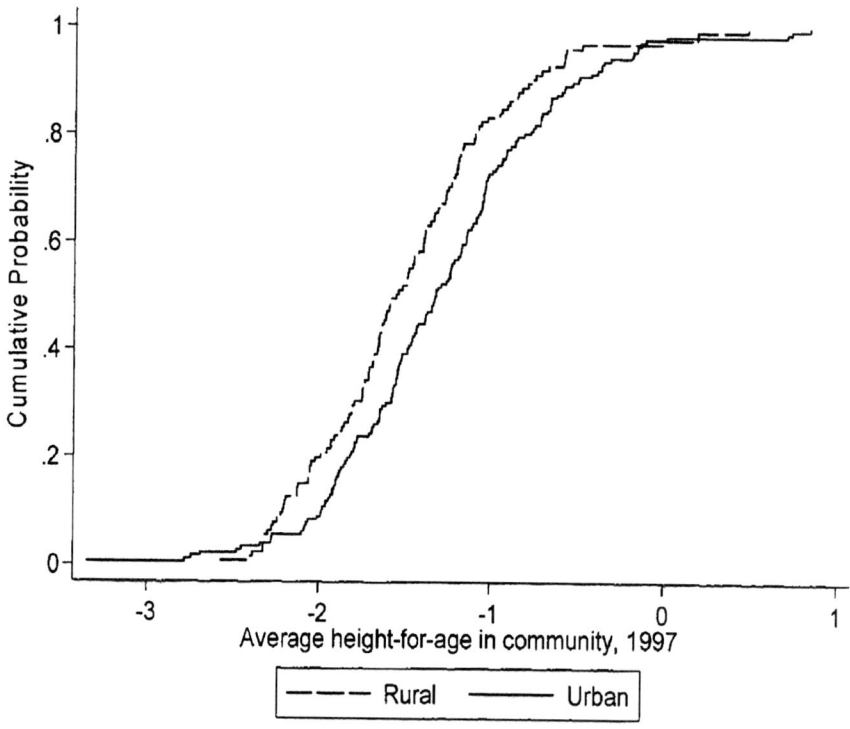

Figure 3.1. CDF of 1997 Community Average Height-for-Age by Location (Rural vs Urban) of Community

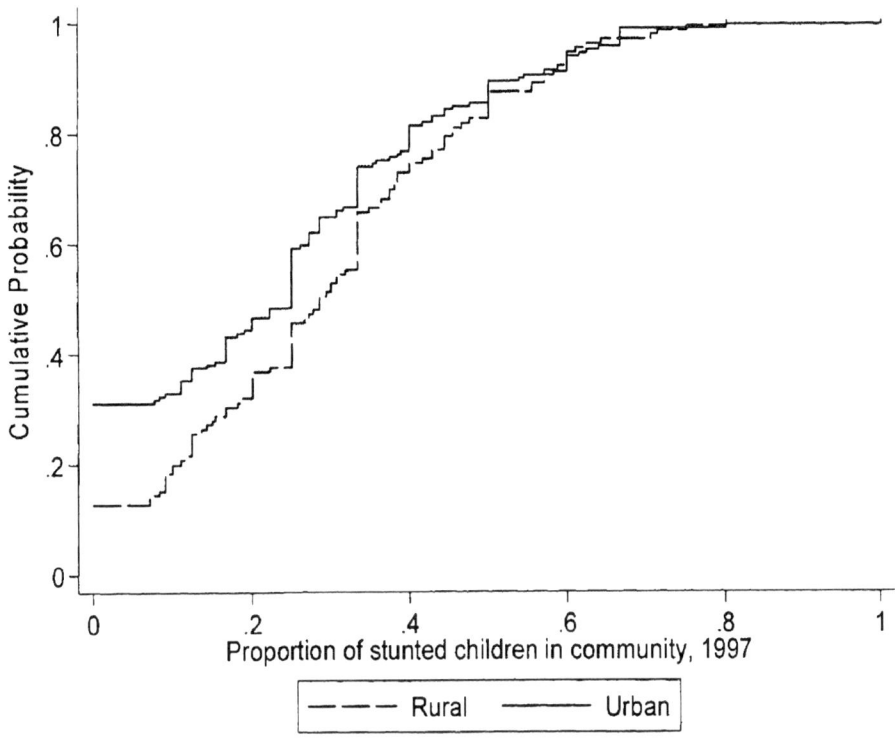

Figure 3.2. CDF of 1997 Stunted Share of Children in Communities by
Community Location (Urban vs Rural).

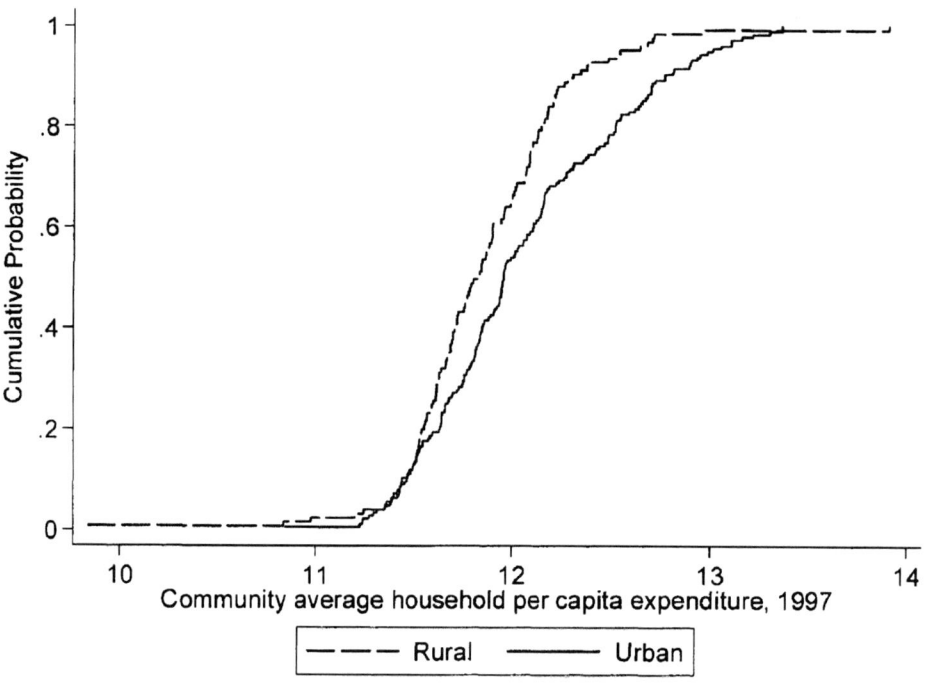

Figure 3.3. CDF of 1997 Average of Household per Capita Expenditure by Community Location.

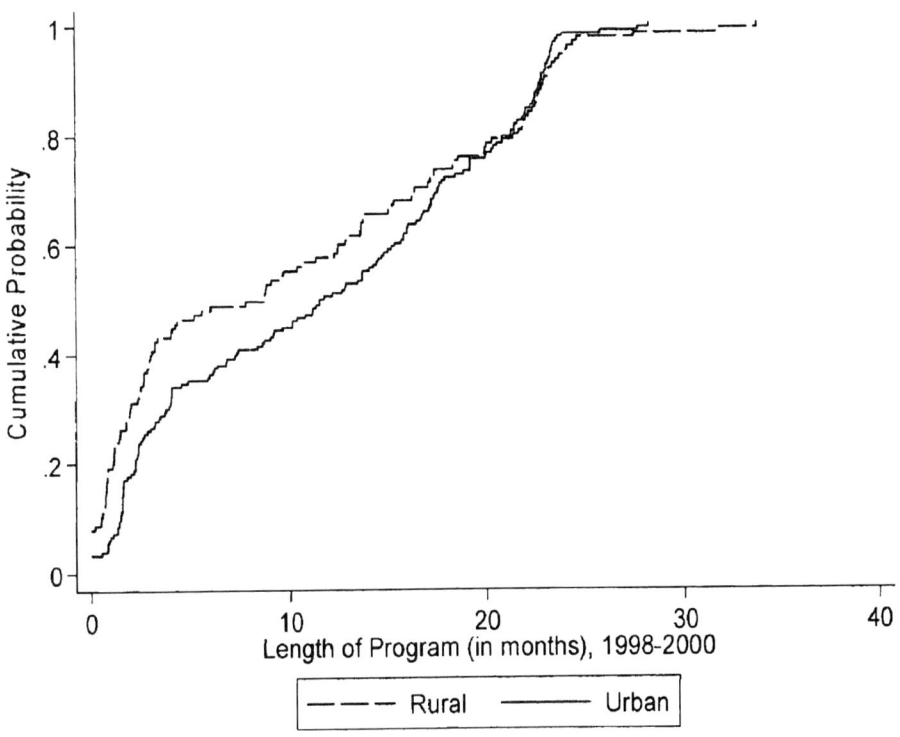

Figure 3.4. CDF of Length of Program in Month by Community Location (Urban vs Rural), 1998-2000.

APPENDICES

Table A3.7.2.1. Impact of PMT on height-for-age of children 6-11 months: binary program variable

	OLS		Fixed-effect	
Year (2000=1)	-0.22	-0.301	-0.41	-0.516
	(0.395)	(0.397)	(0.702)	(0.707)
Program since '98 (Yes=1)*Year	0.248	0.365	0.51	0.62
	(0.384)	(0.387)	(0.711)	(0.723)
Gender (boy=1)	0.103	0.112	0.001	0.002
	(0.124)	(0.124)	(0.198)	(0.208)
Age	-0.127	-0.126	-0.171	-0.171
	(0.036)***	(0.035)***	(0.057)***	(0.058)***
Mother education (years)	0.001	0.001	-0.024	-0.024
	(0.015)	(0.015)	(0.023)	(0.024)
Father education (years)	0.008	0.01	0.014	0.012
	(0.015)	(0.015)	(0.022)	(0.022)
Mother height (cm)	0.061	0.059	0.058	0.055
	(0.012)***	(0.012)***	(0.019)***	(0.019)***
Father height (cm)	0.047	0.049	0.07	0.069
	(0.012)***	(0.012)***	(0.019)***	(0.019)***
Head of HH (male=1)	-0.027	-0.047	0.272	0.273
	(0.222)	(0.221)	(0.444)	(0.463)
Number of children 5-14 yo in HH	0.022	0.019	0.019	0.029
	(0.062)	(0.062)	(0.089)	(0.091)
HH owns private toilet (Yes=1)	0.127	0.087	0.167	0.179
	(0.136)	(0.136)	(0.225)	(0.233)
HH has sanitation (Yes=1)	0.021	-0.048	0.247	0.31
	(0.176)	(0.198)	(0.403)	(0.462)
Per capita income (ln)	0.071	0.094	0.039	0.037
	(0.094)	(0.094)	(0.134)	(0.138)
Type of community (urban=1), C	-	0.336	-	0.065
		(0.169)**		(0.468)
Distance to district capital (km), C	-	0	-	-0.002
		(0.003)		(0.006)
Distance to bus station (km), C	-	0.031	-	0.009
		(0.011)***		(0.022)
Land w/ technical irrigation (%), C	-	-0.001	-	0.275
		(0.333)		(0.840)
Comm. has asphalt road (Yes=1), C	-	-0.251	-	0.001
		(0.163)		(0.393)
Comm. has sewerage system (Yes=1), C	-	0.075	-	-0.294
		(0.140)		(0.343)
Comm. has piped water (Yes=1), C	-	-0.009	-	-0.127
		(0.152)		(0.369)
Constant	-17.655	-18.02	-20.318	-19.585
	(2.558)***	(2.558)***	(3.966)***	(4.050)***
R-squared	0.14	0.16	0.57	0.58

Notes: n is 525. (C) indicates community-level variables. Robust standard errors are in parentheses. (*), (**) and (***) indicate significance respectively at 10%, 5%; and 1%.

Table A3.7.2.2. Impact of PMT on height-for-age of children 12-23 months: binary program variable

	OLS		Fixed-effect	
Year (2000=1)	0.027	-0.02	0.09	0.099
	(0.230)	(0.234)	(0.239)	(0.256)
Program since '98 (Yes=1)*Year	-0.108	-0.052	-0.073	-0.06
	(0.225)	(0.230)	(0.265)	(0.280)
Gender (boy=1)	-0.136	-0.138	-0.211	-0.206
	(0.075)*	(0.075)*	(0.089)**	(0.090)**
Age	-0.043	-0.043	-0.033	-0.034
	(0.011)***	(0.011)***	(0.012)***	(0.012)***
Mother education (years)	0.005	0.005	-0.008	-0.008
	(0.009)	(0.009)	(0.009)	(0.009)
Father education (years)	0.003	0.002	0.001	0.001
	(0.009)	(0.009)	(0.010)	(0.010)
Mother height (cm)	0.023	0.022	0.028	0.028
	(0.007)***	(0.007)***	(0.008)***	(0.008)***
Father height (cm)	0.031	0.031	0.037	0.037
	(0.008)***	(0.008)***	(0.009)***	(0.009)***
Head of HH (male=1)	-0.013	-0.002	-0.147	-0.153
	(0.123)	(0.123)	(0.135)	(0.138)
Number of children 5-14 yo in HH	0.006	0.011	0.028	0.027
	(0.037)	(0.038)	(0.045)	(0.045)
HH owns private toilet (Yes=1)	0.106	0.104	0.12	0.118
	(0.081)	(0.081)	(0.106)	(0.107)
HH has sanitation (Yes=1)	0.164	0.141	0.076	0.053
	(0.099)*	(0.114)	(0.161)	(0.171)
Per capita income (ln)	0.157	0.161	0.105	0.101
	(0.061)***	(0.061)***	(0.073)	(0.073)
Type of community (urban=1), C	-	0.13	-	0.159
		(0.104)		(0.212)
Distance to district capital (km), C	-	-0.001	-	0
		(0.002)		(0.003)
Distance to bus station (km), C	-	0.01	-	0.016
		(0.006)		(0.012)
Land w/ technical irrigation (%), C	-	0.393	-	-0.28
		(0.210)*		(0.429)
Comm. has asphalt road (Yes=1), C	-	-0.118	-	0.006
		(0.103)		(0.189)
Comm. has sewerage system (Yes=1), C	-	-0.08	-	-0.081
		(0.086)		(0.165)
Comm. has piped water (Yes=1), C	-	0.077	-	0.005
		(0.093)		(0.161)
Constant	-11.754	-11.677	-12.728	-12.817
	(1.696)***	(1.708)***	(1.964)***	(1.991)***
R-squared	0.08	0.08	0.40	0.40

Notes: n is 1042. (C) indicates community-level variables. Robust standard errors are in parentheses. (*), (**) and (***) indicate significance respectively at 10%, 5%; and 1%.

Table A3.7.2.3. Impact of PMT on height-for-age of children 24-59 months: binary program variable

	OLS		Fixed-effect	
Year (2000=1)	0.074	0.102	0.114	0.126
	(0.136)	(0.137)	(0.186)	(0.186)
Program since '98 (Yes=1)*Year	-0.135	-0.157	-0.138	-0.153
	(0.133)	(0.134)	(0.190)	(0.191)
Gender (boy=1)	-0.01	-0.008	-0.001	-0.002
	(0.040)	(0.040)	(0.041)	(0.041)
Age	0.005	0.005	0.004	0.004
	(0.002)***	(0.002)***	(0.002)**	(0.002)**
Mother education (years)	0.017	0.016	0.011	0.011
	(0.005)***	(0.005)***	(0.005)**	(0.005)**
Father education (years)	-0.005	-0.006	-0.003	-0.003
	(0.005)	(0.005)	(0.005)	(0.005)
Mother height (cm)	0.054	0.053	0.052	0.053
	(0.004)***	(0.004)***	(0.004)***	(0.004)***
Father height (cm)	0.032	0.032	0.032	0.033
	(0.004)***	(0.004)***	(0.004)***	(0.004)***
Head of HH (male=1)	0.016	0.02	-0.031	-0.023
	(0.067)	(0.067)	(0.068)	(0.069)
Number of children 5-14 yo in HH	-0.043	-0.041	-0.019	-0.019
	(0.019)**	(0.019)**	(0.021)	(0.021)
HH owns private toilet (Yes=1)	0.101	0.087	0.074	0.068
	(0.044)**	(0.044)**	(0.048)	(0.049)
HH has sanitation (Yes=1)	0.319	0.252	0.311	0.281
	(0.055)***	(0.064)***	(0.071)***	(0.075)***
Per capita income (ln)	0.158	0.155	0.156	0.153
	(0.031)***	(0.031)***	(0.035)***	(0.035)***
Type of community (urban=1), C	-	0.138	-	-0.037
		(0.058)**		(0.092)
Distance to district capital (km), C	-	-0.001	-	-0.002
		(0.001)		(0.001)
Distance to bus station (km), C	-	0.002	-	0.002
		(0.003)		(0.005)
Land w/ technical irrigation (%), C	-	0.018	-	-0.168
		(0.114)		(0.182)
Comm. has asphalt road (Yes=1), C	-	-0.019	-	0.183
		(0.053)		(0.086)**
Comm. has sewerage system (Yes=1), C	-	-0.054	-	0.012
		(0.047)		(0.076)
Comm. has piped water (Yes=1), C	-	0.005	-	-0.002
		(0.049)		(0.077)
Constant	-17.011	-16.763	-16.716	-16.869
	(0.848)***	(0.854)***	(0.933)***	(0.952)***
R-squared	0.15	0.15	0.27	0.27

Notes: n is 3221. (C) indicates community-level variables. Robust standard errors are in parentheses. (*), (**) and (***) indicate significance respectively at 10%, 5%; and 1%

Table A3.7.2.4. Impact of PMT on probability of children (6-11 months) being stunted: binary program variable

	OLS		Fixed-effect	
Year (2000=1)	0.07	0.085	0.223	0.277
	(0.107)	(0.108)	(0.199)	(0.204)
Program since '98 (Yes=1)*Year	-0.124	-0.144	-0.332	-0.399
	(0.104)	(0.105)	(0.196)*	(0.202)**
Gender (boy=1)	-0.025	-0.025	0.021	0.025
	(0.033)	(0.034)	(0.054)	(0.056)
Age	0.024	0.023	0.019	0.021
	(0.010)**	(0.010)**	(0.017)	(0.017)
Mother education (years)	0.003	0.003	0.01	0.01
	(0.004)	(0.004)	(0.007)	(0.007)
Father education (years)	0.000	0.000	-0.001	-0.001
	(0.004)	(0.004)	(0.006)	(0.006)
Mother height (cm)	-0.011	-0.011	-0.01	-0.009
	(0.003)***	(0.003)***	(0.005)*	(0.005)*
Father height (cm)	-0.014	-0.014	-0.021	-0.02
	(0.003)***	(0.003)***	(0.005)***	(0.005)***
Head of HH (male=1)	0.016	0.014	0.003	-0.005
	(0.060)	(0.060)	(0.116)	(0.120)
Number of children 5-14 yo in HH	0.009	0.010	0.008	0.006
	(0.017)	(0.017)	(0.025)	(0.025)
HH owns private toilet (Yes=1)	-0.046	-0.04	-0.075	-0.074
	(0.037)	(0.037)	(0.058)	(0.060)
HH has sanitation (Yes=1)	0.031	0.023	0.019	-0.011
	(0.048)	(0.054)	(0.109)	(0.131)
Per capita income (ln)	-0.029	-0.034	-0.033	-0.039
	(0.025)	(0.026)	(0.039)	(0.040)
Type of community (urban=1), C	-	-0.025	-	-0.004
		(0.046)		(0.128)
Distance to district capital (km), C	-	0.000	-	0.001
		(0.001)		(0.002)
Distance to bus station (km), C	-	-0.005	-	-0.002
		(0.003)*		(0.006)
Land w/ technical irrigation (%), C	-	-0.061	-	-0.359
		(0.091)		(0.222)
Comm. has asphalt road (Yes=1), C	-	0.033	-	0.001
		(0.044)		(0.115)
Comm. has sewerage system (Yes=1), C	-	-0.042	-	0.044
		(0.038)		(0.098)
Comm. has piped water (Yes=1), C	-	0.032	-	-0.014
		(0.041)		(0.088)
Constant	4.119	4.196	5.338	5.103
	(0.690)***	(0.696)***	(1.145)***	(1.189)***
R-squared	0.10	0.11	0.53	0.54

Notes: n is 525. (C) indicates community-level variables. Robust standard errors are in parentheses. (*), (**) and (***) indicate significance respectively at 10%, 5%; and 1%.

Table A3.7.2.5. Impact of PMT on probability of children (12-23 months) being stunted: binary program variable

	OLS		Fixed-effect	
Year (2000=1)	-0.076	-0.058	0.02	0.044
	(0.087)	(0.088)	(0.149)	(0.152)
Program since '98 (Yes=1)*Year	0.019	-0.007	-0.099	-0.123
	(0.085)	(0.087)	(0.154)	(0.158)
Gender (boy=1)	0.042	0.041	0.071	0.075
	(0.028)	(0.028)	(0.034)**	(0.035)**
Age	0.007	0.008	0.002	0.001
	(0.004)*	(0.004)*	(0.005)	(0.005)
Mother education (years)	0.000	0.000	0.004	0.005
	(0.003)	(0.003)	(0.004)	(0.004)
Father education (years)	0.000	0.001	0.001	0.002
	(0.003)	(0.003)	(0.004)	(0.004)
Mother height (cm)	-0.01	-0.01	-0.013	-0.013
	(0.003)***	(0.003)***	(0.003)***	(0.003)***
Father height (cm)	-0.01	-0.011	-0.012	-0.012
	(0.003)***	(0.003)***	(0.003)***	(0.003)***
Head of HH (male=1)	-0.013	-0.015	0.068	0.069
	(0.047)	(0.047)	(0.058)	(0.059)
Number of children 5-14 yo in HH	-0.003	-0.005	-0.014	-0.014
	(0.014)	(0.014)	(0.017)	(0.017)
HH owns private toilet (Yes=1)	-0.053	-0.05	-0.048	-0.043
	(0.031)*	(0.031)	(0.041)	(0.042)
HH has sanitation (Yes=1)	-0.111	-0.078	0.009	0.023
	(0.038)***	(0.043)*	(0.061)	(0.065)
Per capita income (ln)	-0.041	-0.045	-0.053	-0.052
	(0.023)*	(0.023)*	(0.029)*	(0.029)*
Type of community (urban=1), C	-	-0.036	-	0.009
		(0.039)		(0.076)
Distance to district capital (km), C	-	0.000	-	0.001
		(0.001)		(0.001)
Distance to bus station (km), C	-	-0.004	-	-0.001
		(0.002)*		(0.005)
Land w/ technical irrigation (%), C	-	-0.128	-	0.001
		(0.080)		(0.143)
Comm. has asphalt road (Yes=1), C	-	0.034	-	-0.089
		(0.039)		(0.073)
Comm. has sewerage system (Yes=1), C	-	-0.034	-	0.031
		(0.033)		(0.058)
Comm. has piped water (Yes=1), C	-	-0.04	-	-0.062
		(0.035)		(0.066)
Constant	3.996	4.072	4.787	4.833
	(0.641)***	(0.645)***	(0.744)***	(0.750)***
R-squared	0.08	0.09	0.38	0.38

Notes: n is 1042. (C) indicates community-level variables. Robust standard errors are in parentheses. (*), (**) and (***) indicate significance respectively at 10%, 5%; and 1%.

Table A3.7.2.6. Impact of PMT on probability of children (24-59 months) being stunted: binary program variable

	OLS		Fixed-effect	
Year (2000=1)	-0.008	-0.014	-0.037	-0.039
	(0.053)	(0.054)	(0.071)	(0.071)
Program since '98 (Yes=1)*Year	0.013	0.019	0.045	0.049
	(0.052)	(0.053)	(0.072)	(0.072)
Gender (boy=1)	0.013	0.013	0.004	0.005
	(0.016)	(0.016)	(0.016)	(0.016)
Age	-0.003	-0.003	-0.003	-0.003
	(0.001)***	(0.001)***	(0.001)***	(0.001)***
Mother education (years)	-0.005	-0.005	-0.005	-0.005
	(0.002)***	(0.002)***	(0.002)**	(0.002)**
Father education (years)	0.001	0.001	0.001	0.001
	(0.002)	(0.002)	(0.002)	(0.002)
Mother height (cm)	-0.018	-0.017	-0.017	-0.017
	(0.002)***	(0.002)***	(0.002)***	(0.002)***
Father height (cm)	-0.01	-0.01	-0.01	-0.011
	(0.002)***	(0.002)***	(0.002)***	(0.002)***
Head of HH (male=1)	0.000	-0.002	0.012	0.011
	(0.026)	(0.026)	(0.028)	(0.028)
Number of children 5-14 yo in HH	0.019	0.017	0.014	0.014
	(0.008)**	(0.008)**	(0.008)*	(0.008)*
HH owns private toilet (Yes=1)	-0.027	-0.025	-0.025	-0.025
	(0.017)	(0.017)	(0.020)	(0.020)
HH has sanitation (Yes=1)	-0.091	-0.077	-0.08	-0.082
	(0.022)***	(0.025)***	(0.027)***	(0.029)***
Per capita income (ln)	-0.053	-0.051	-0.057	-0.057
	(0.012)***	(0.012)***	(0.013)***	(0.013)***
Type of community (urban=1), C	-	-0.041	-	0.022
		(0.023)*		(0.038)
Distance to district capital (km), C	-	0	-	0
		(0.000)		(0.001)
Distance to bus station (km), C	-	-0.001	-	0
		(0.001)		(0.002)
Land w/ technical irrigation (%), C	-	-0.06	-	-0.032
		(0.045)		(0.069)
Comm. has asphalt road (Yes=1), C	-	-0.016	-	-0.068
		(0.021)		(0.035)*
Comm. has sewerage system (Yes=1), C	-	0.028	-	-0.008
		(0.018)		(0.029)
Comm. has piped water (Yes=1), C	-	0.004	-	0.003
		(0.019)		(0.029)
Constant	5.401	5.305	5.325	5.394
	(0.333)***	(0.336)***	(0.366)***	(0.373)***
R-squared	0.11	0.12	0.22	0.22

Notes: n is 3221. (C) indicates community-level variables. Robust standard errors are in parentheses. (*), (**) and (***) indicate significance respectively at 10%, 5%; and 1%

Table A3.7.2.7. Impact of PMT on height-for-age of children 6-11 months proportion of child age exposed to the program

	OLS		Fixed-effect	
Year (2000=1)	0 044	0 118	-0 036	-0 052
	(0 172)	(0 173)	(0 343)	(0 358)
Age exposed to the program*Year	-0 048	-0 128	0 219	0 24
	(0 187)	(0 190)	(0 477)	(0 501)
Gender (boy=1)	0 107	0 118	-0 01	-0 009
	(0 124)	(0 124)	(0 198)	(0 208)
Age	-0 129	-0 129	-0 172	-0 172
	(0 036)***	(0 035)***	(0 057)***	(0 058)***
Mother education (years)	0 001	0 001	-0 025	-0 024
	(0 015)	(0 015)	(0 022)	(0 024)
Father education (years)	0 007	0 009	0 013	0 011
	(0 015)	(0 015)	(0 022)	(0 022)
Mother height (cm)	0 061	0 059	0 059	0 057
	(0 012)***	(0 012)***	(0 019)***	(0 019)***
Father height (cm)	0 047	0 048	0 07	0 069
	(0 012)***	(0 012)***	(0 019)***	(0 019)***
Head of HH (male=1)	-0 041	-0 072	0 278	0 276
	(0 222)	(0 221)	(0 443)	(0 461)
Number of children 5-14 yo in HH	0 024	0 022	0 021	0 03
	(0 062)	(0 062)	(0 089)	(0 091)
HH owns private toilet (Yes=1)	0 113	0 061	0 174	0 185
	(0 136)	(0 137)	(0 224)	(0 232)
HH has sanitation (Yes=1)	0 027	-0 043	0 238	0 303
	(0 177)	(0 198)	(0 395)	(0 453)
Per capita income (ln)	0 075	0 100	0 037	0 034
	(0 094)	(0 094)	(0 134)	(0 138)
Type of community (urban=1), C	-	0 362	-	0 084
		(0 170)**		(0 462)
Distance to district capital (km), C	-	0 000	-	-0 002
		(0 003)		(0 006)
Distance to bus station (km), C	-	0 029	-	0 007
		(0 011)***		(0 022)
Land w/ technical irrigation (%), C	-	-0 019	-	0 229
		(0 335)		(0 849)
Comm has asphalt road (Yes=1), C	-	-0 265	-	-0 023
		(0 164)		(0 385)
Comm has sewerage system (Yes=1), C	-	0 07	-	-0 267
		(0 140)		(0 341)
Comm has piped water (Yes=1), C	-	-0 021	-	-0 168
		(0 152)		(0 358)
Constant	-17 656	-17 979	-20 413	-19 717
	(2 559)***	(2 558)***	(3 929)***	(4 035)***
R-squared	0 14	0 16	0 57	0 58

Notes n is 525 (C) indicates community-level variables Robust standard errors are in parentheses. (*), (**) and (***) indicate significance respectively at 10%, 5%, and 1%

Table A3.7.2.8. Impact of PMT on height-for-age of children 12-23 months: proportion of child age exposed to the program

	OLS		Fixed-effect	
Year (2000=1)	-0.093	-0.089	-0.213	-0.227
	(0.104)	(0.105)	(0.145)	(0.152)
Age exposed to the program*Year	0.035	0.04	0.482	0.552
	(0.125)	(0.126)	(0.229)**	(0.237)**
Gender (boy=1)	-0.137	-0.139	-0.223	-0.219
	(0.074)*	(0.074)*	(0.088)**	(0.089)**
Age	-0.042	-0.043	-0.029	-0.029
	(0.011)***	(0.011)***	(0.012)**	(0.012)**
Mother education (years)	0.005	0.005	-0.009	-0.009
	(0.009)	(0.009)	(0.009)	(0.009)
Father education (years)	0.003	0.002	0.000	0.000
	(0.009)	(0.009)	(0.010)	(0.010)
Mother height (cm)	0.023	0.022	0.027	0.027
	(0.007)***	(0.007)***	(0.008)***	(0.008)***
Father height (cm)	0.031	0.031	0.035	0.035
	(0.008)***	(0.008)***	(0.009)***	(0.009)***
Head of HH (male=1)	-0.011	-0.001	-0.158	-0.167
	(0.123)	(0.123)	(0.135)	(0.138)
Number of children 5-14 yo in HH	0.007	0.011	0.033	0.031
	(0.037)	(0.038)	(0.044)	(0.045)
HH owns private toilet (Yes=1)	0.107	0.105	0.091	0.09
	(0.081)	(0.081)	(0.105)	(0.105)
HH has sanitation (Yes=1)	0.168	0.146	0.098	0.099
	(0.100)*	(0.114)	(0.159)	(0.167)
Per capita income (ln)	0.157	0.161	0.115	0.114
	(0.061)**	(0.061)***	(0.072)	(0.072)
Type of community (urban=1), C	-	0.125	-	0.093
		(0.104)		(0.214)
Distance to district capital (km), C	-	-0.001	-	0.001
		(0.002)		(0.003)
Distance to bus station (km), C	-	0.011	-	0.018
		(0.006)*		(0.012)
Land w/ technical irrigation (%), C	-	0.396	-	-0.36
		(0.211)*		(0.426)
Comm. has asphalt road (Yes=1), C	-	-0.116	-	0.07
		(0.103)		(0.187)
Comm. has sewerage system (Yes=1), C	-	-0.079	-	-0.075
		(0.086)		(0.163)
Comm. has piped water (Yes=1), C	-	0.079	-	-0.03
		(0.093)		(0.162)
Constant	-11.671	-11.627	-12.423	-12.555
	(1.698)***	(1.710)***	(1.957)***	(1.982)***
R-squared	0.08	0.09	0.41	0.41

Notes: n is 1042. (C) indicates community-level variables. Robust standard errors are in parentheses. (*), (**) and (***) indicate significance respectively at 10%, 5%; and 1%.

Table A3.7.2.9. Impact of PMT on height-for-age of children 24-59 months: proportion of child age exposed to the program

	OLS		Fixed-effect	
Year (2000=1)	-0.023	-0.009	0.009	0.002
	(0.058)	(0.058)	(0.071)	(0.073)
Age exposed to the program*Year	-0.12	-0.143	-0.095	-0.072
	(0.117)	(0.118)	(0.171)	(0.174)
Gender (boy=1)	-0.01	-0.008	-0.001	-0.003
	(0.040)	(0.040)	(0.041)	(0.041)
Age	0.005	0.005	0.004	0.004
	(0.002)**	(0.002)**	(0.002)*	(0.002)*
Mother education (years)	0.017	0.017	0.011	0.011
	(0.005)***	(0.005)***	(0.005)**	(0.005)**
Father education (years)	-0.005	-0.006	-0.003	-0.003
	(0.005)	(0.005)	(0.005)	(0.005)
Mother height (cm)	0.054	0.053	0.052	0.053
	(0.004)***	(0.004)***	(0.004)***	(0.004)***
Father height (cm)	0.032	0.032	0.032	0.033
	(0.004)***	(0.004)***	(0.004)***	(0.004)***
Head of HH (male=1)	0.018	0.023	-0.03	-0.022
	(0.066)	(0.067)	(0.068)	(0.069)
Number of children 5-14 yo in HH	-0.043	-0.04	-0.019	-0.019
	(0.019)**	(0.019)**	(0.021)	(0.021)
HH owns private toilet (Yes=1)	0.104	0.09	0.074	0.068
	(0.044)**	(0.044)**	(0.048)	(0.049)
HH has sanitation (Yes=1)	0.318	0.25	0.312	0.281
	(0.055)***	(0.064)***	(0.071)***	(0.075)***
Per capita income (ln)	0.157	0.155	0.156	0.153
	(0.031)***	(0.031)***	(0.035)***	(0.035)***
Type of community (urban=1), C	-	0.14	-	-0.034
		(0.058)**		(0.093)
Distance to district capital (km), C	-	-0.001	-	-0.002
		(0.001)		(0.001)
Distance to bus station (km), C	-	0.003	-	0.003
		(0.003)		(0.005)
Land w/ technical irrigation (%), C	-	0.01	-	-0.161
		(0.115)		(0.182)
Comm. has asphalt road (Yes=1), C	-	-0.021	-	0.178
		(0.053)		(0.086)**
Comm. has sewerage system (Yes=1), C	-	-0.056	-	0.011
		(0.047)		(0.076)
Comm. has piped water (Yes=1), C	-	0.007	-	0.005
		(0.049)		(0.078)
Constant	-17.016	-16.775	-16.706	-16.862
	(0.848)***	(0.854)***	(0.933)***	(0.952)***
R-squared	0.15	0.15	0.27	0.27

Notes: n is 3221. (C) indicates community-level variables. Robust standard errors are in parentheses. (*), (**) and (***) indicate significance respectively at 10%, 5%; and 1%

Table A3.7.2.10. Impact of PMT on probability of children (6-11 months) being stunted: proportion of child age exposed to the program

	OLS		Fixed-effect	
Year (2000=1)	-0.052	-0.06	-0.064	-0.061
	(0.047)	(0.047)	(0.100)	(0.103)
Age exposed to the program*Year	0.006	0.012	-0.061	-0.08
	(0.051)	(0.052)	(0.130)	(0.134)
Gender (boy=1)	-0.027	-0.027	0.026	0.03
	(0.033)	(0.034)	(0.054)	(0.056)
Age	0.024	0.024	0.019	0.021
	(0.010)**	(0.010)**	(0.017)	(0.017)
Mother education (years)	0.003	0.003	0.01	0.011
	(0.004)	(0.004)	(0.007)	(0.007)
Father education (years)	0.000	0.000	-0.001	0.000
	(0.004)	(0.004)	(0.006)	(0.006)
Mother height (cm)	-0.011	-0.011	-0.011	-0.01
	(0.003)***	(0.003)***	(0.005)**	(0.005)*
Father height (cm)	-0.013	-0.013	-0.021	-0.02
	(0.003)***	(0.003)***	(0.005)***	(0.006)***
Head of HH (male=1)	0.022	0.021	0.004	-0.002
	(0.060)	(0.060)	(0.115)	(0.118)
Number of children 5-14 yo in HH	0.008	0.009	0.006	0.005
	(0.017)	(0.017)	(0.026)	(0.026)
HH owns private toilet (Yes=1)	-0.041	-0.033	-0.077	-0.075
	(0.037)	(0.037)	(0.059)	(0.060)
HH has sanitation (Yes=1)	0.03	0.023	0.018	-0.01
	(0.048)	(0.054)	(0.108)	(0.129)
Per capita income (ln)	-0.03	-0.036	-0.032	-0.037
	(0.025)	(0.026)	(0.039)	(0.040)
Type of community (urban=1), C	-	-0.03	-	-0.019
		(0.046)		(0.129)
Distance to district capital (km), C	-	0	-	0
		(0.001)		(0.002)
Distance to bus station (km), C	-	-0.005	-	-0.001
		(0.003)		(0.006)
Land w/ technical irrigation (%), C	-	-0.061	-	-0.312
		(0.091)		(0.225)
Comm. has asphalt road (Yes=1), C	-	0.035	-	0.02
		(0.045)		(0.115)
Comm. has sewerage system (Yes=1), C	-	-0.041	-	0.026
		(0.038)		(0.098)
Comm. has piped water (Yes=1), C	-	0.037	-	0.012
		(0.041)		(0.090)
Constant	4.117	4.178	5.392	5.167
	(0.691)***	(0.697)***	(1.140)***	(1.192)***
R-squared	0.09	0.11	0.52	0.53

Notes: n is 525. (C) indicates community-level variables. Robust standard errors are in parentheses. (*), (**) and (***) indicate significance respectively at 10%, 5%; and 1%.

Table A3.7.2.11. Impact of PMT on probability of children (12-23 months) being stunted: proportion of child age exposed to the program

	OLS		Fixed-effect	
Year (2000=1)	-0.072	-0.079	0.003	0.006
	(0.039)*	(0.040)**	(0.053)	(0.056)
Age exposed to the program*Year	0.028	0.028	-0.154	-0.155
	(0.047)	(0.048)	(0.082)*	(0.084)*
Gender (boy=1)	0.041	0.041	0.074	0.077
	(0.028)	(0.028)	(0.034)**	(0.035)**
Age	0.008	0.008	0.001	0.000
	(0.004)*	(0.004)*	(0.005)	(0.005)
Mother education (years)	0.000	0.000	0.005	0.005
	(0.003)	(0.003)	(0.004)	(0.004)
Father education (years)	0.000	0.001	0.001	0.001
	(0.003)	(0.003)	(0.004)	(0.004)
Mother height (cm)	-0.010	-0.010	-0.013	-0.013
	(0.003)***	(0.003)***	(0.003)***	(0.003)***
Father height (cm)	-0.011	-0.011	-0.011	-0.011
	(0.003)***	(0.003)***	(0.003)***	(0.003)***
Head of HH (male=1)	-0.012	-0.015	0.071	0.071
	(0.047)	(0.047)	(0.058)	(0.059)
Number of children 5-14 yo in HH	-0.003	-0.005	-0.015	-0.015
	(0.014)	(0.014)	(0.017)	(0.017)
HH owns private toilet (Yes=1)	-0.054	-0.050	-0.041	-0.038
	(0.031)*	(0.031)	(0.041)	(0.042)
HH has sanitation (Yes=1)	-0.110	-0.075	0.006	0.014
	(0.038)***	(0.043)*	(0.061)	(0.064)
Per capita income (ln)	-0.042	-0.045	-0.055	-0.055
	(0.023)*	(0.023)*	(0.029)*	(0.029)*
Type of community (urban=1), C	-	-0.039	-	0.025
		(0.039)		(0.075)
Distance to district capital (km), C	-	0.000	-	0.000
		(0.001)		(0.001)
Distance to bus station (km), C	-	-0.004	-	-0.001
		(0.002)		(0.005)
Land w/ technical irrigation (%), C	-	-0.126	-	0.035
		(0.080)		(0.144)
Comm. has asphalt road (Yes=1), C	-	0.035	-	-0.104
		(0.039)		(0.074)
Comm. has sewerage system (Yes=1), C	-	-0.034	-	0.030
		(0.033)		(0.058)
Comm. has piped water (Yes=1), C	-	-0.040	-	-0.048
		(0.035)		(0.066)
Constant	4.017	4.099	4.714	4.774
	(0.642)***	(0.646)***	(0.742)***	(0.747)***
R-squared	0.08	0.09	0.38	0.38

Notes: n is 1042. (C) indicates community-level variables. Robust standard errors are in parentheses. (*), (**) and (***) indicate significance respectively at 10%, 5%; and 1%.

Table A3.7.2.12. Impact of PMT on probability of children (24-59 months) being stunted: proportion of child age exposed to the program

	OLS		Fixed-effect	
Year (2000=1)	-0.009	-0.01	-0.014	-0.01
	(0.023)	(0.023)	(0.027)	(0.028)
Age exposed to the program*Year	0.049	0.053	0.075	0.062
	(0.046)	(0.046)	(0.068)	(0.069)
Gender (boy=1)	0.013	0.013	0.004	0.005
	(0.016)	(0.016)	(0.016)	(0.016)
Age	-0.003	-0.003	-0.003	-0.003
	(0.001)***	(0.001)***	(0.001)***	(0.001)***
Mother education (years)	-0.005	-0.005	-0.005	-0.005
	(0.002)***	(0.002)***	(0.002)**	(0.002)**
Father education (years)	0.001	0.001	0.001	0.001
	(0.002)	(0.002)	(0.002)	(0.002)
Mother height (cm)	-0.018	-0.018	-0.017	-0.017
	(0.002)***	(0.002)***	(0.002)***	(0.002)***
Father height (cm)	-0.01	-0.01	-0.01	-0.011
	(0.002)***	(0.002)***	(0.002)***	(0.002)***
Head of HH (male=1)	-0.001	-0.003	0.012	0.011
	(0.026)	(0.026)	(0.028)	(0.028)
Number of children 5-14 yo in HH	0.019	0.017	0.014	0.014
	(0.008)**	(0.008)**	(0.008)*	(0.008)*
HH owns private toilet (Yes=1)	-0.027	-0.025	-0.025	-0.025
	(0.017)	(0.017)	(0.020)	(0.020)
HH has sanitation (Yes=1)	-0.09	-0.076	-0.081	-0.081
	(0.022)***	(0.025)***	(0.027)***	(0.029)***
Per capita income (ln)	-0.053	-0.051	-0.057	-0.057
	(0.012)***	(0.012)***	(0.013)***	(0.013)***
Type of community (urban=1), C	-	-0.043	-	0.018
		(0.023)*		(0.038)
Distance to district capital (km), C	-	0.000	-	0.000
		(0.000)		(0.001)
Distance to bus station (km), C	-	-0.001	-	-0.001
		(0.001)		(0.002)
Land w/ technical irrigation (%), C	-	-0.056	-	-0.034
		(0.045)		(0.069)
Comm. has asphalt road (Yes=1), C	-	-0.015	-	-0.064
		(0.021)		(0.035)*
Comm. has sewerage system (Yes=1), C	-	0.029	-	-0.007
		(0.018)		(0.029)
Comm. has piped water (Yes=1), C	-	0.004	-	0.001
		(0.019)		(0.029)
Constant	5.405	5.309	5.324	5.39
	(0.333)***	(0.336)***	(0.366)***	(0.373)***
R-squared	0.11	0.12	0.22	0.22

Notes: n is 3221. (C) indicates community-level variables. Robust standard errors are in parentheses. (*), (**) and (***) indicate significance respectively at 10%, 5%; and 1%.

BIBLIOGRAPHY

BIBLIOGRAPHY

Alderman, Harold, Behrman, Jere R., Lavy, Victor and Menon, Rekha. (2001) Child Health and school enrollment: A longitudinal analysis. *Journal of Human Resources*, 31(1):185-205.

Alderman, Harold and Behrman, Jere R. (2006). Reducing the incidence of low birth weight in low-income countries has substantial economic benefits. *World Bank Research Observer*, 21(1).25-48.

Alderman, Harold, Hoddinott, John and Kinsey, William. (2006). Long-term consequences of early childhood malnutrition. *Oxford Economic Papers*, 58(3):450-474.

Alderman, Harold, Hoogeven, Hans, and Rossi, Mariacristina (2009). Preschool Nutrition and Subsequent Schooling Attainment. *Economic Development and Cultural Change*, 57: 239-360

Armecin, Graeme, Behrman, Jere R., Duazo, Paulita, Ghuman, Sharon, Gultiano, Socorro, King, Elizabeth and Lee, Nannette. (2006). Early Childhood Development Through an Integrated Program: Evidence from the Philippines. *World Bank Policy Research Working Paper No.*

Baum, C.F., Schaffer, M.E., and Stillman, S. (2003). Instrumental Variables and GMM: Estimation and testing. *The Stata Journal*, 3(1):1-31.

Baum, C.F., Schaffer, M.E., and Stillman, S. (2007). Enhanced routines for instrumental variables/GMM estimation and testing. *The Stata Journal*, 7(4):465-506.

Behrman, Jere (1996). The impact of health and nutrition on education. *World Bank Research Observer*, 11(1):23-38.

Behrman, J., Cheng, Y. and Todd, P.E. (2004). Evaluating Preschool Programs When Length of Exposure to the Program Varies: A Nonparametric Approach. *Review of Economics and Statistics*, 86/1, 108-132.

Behrman, Jere R., and Lavy, Victor. (1998). *Child Health and Schooling Achievement: Association, Causality and Household Allocations*. Philadelphia: University of Pennsylvania. Mimeo.

Behrman, Jere R. and Rosenzweig, Mark R. (2004). Returns to birthweight. *Review of Economics and Statistics*, 86(2):586-601.

Behrman, Jere R., Hoddinott, John, Maluccio, John, Soler-Hampejsek, Erica, Behrman, Emily L., Martorell, Reynaldo, Ramirez-Zea, Manuel and Stein, Aryeh. (2006). *What determines adult cognitive skills? Impacts of pre-schooling, schooling and post-schooling experiences in Guatemala.* Department of Economics, University of Pennsylvania, Mimeo.

Frankenber, Elizabeth and Karoly, Lynn. (1995). *The 1993 Indonesia Family Life Survey: Overview and field report.* Santa Monica: RAND.

Duflo, E., (2001). Schooling and Labor Market Consequences of School Construction in Indonesia: Evidence from an Unusual Policy Experiment, , *American Economic Review*, 91/4, 795-813

Duflo, E., Glennerster, R., Kremer, M., (2007). Using Randomization in Development Economics Research: A Tool Kit. In Schultz, P., and Strauss, J., eds, *Handbook of Development Economics, Volume 4*, Amsterdam: North Holland Press.

Frankenberg, Elizabeth, (1995). The Effects of Access to Health Care on Infant Mortality in Indonesia. *Health Transition Review*, 5, 143-163.

Frankenberg, E., Thomas, D. and Beegle, K. (1999). The Real Cost of Indonesia's Economic Crisis: Preliminary Findings from the Indonesia Family Life Surveys. *Labor and Population Program Working Papers Series 99-04*, RAND, Santa-Monica.

Frankenberg, Elizabeth and Thomas, Duncan. (2000). *The Indonesia Family Life Survey (IFLS): Study design and Results from waves 1 and 2.* Santa Monica: RAND.

Frankenberg, Elizabeth and Thomas, Duncan (2001). Women's health and pregnancy outcomes: Do services make a difference. *Demography*, 38(2):253-265.

Frankenberg, Elizabeth, Suriastini, Wayan and Thomas, Duncan (2005). Can expanding access to basic healthcare improve children's health status? Lessons from Indonesia's 'midwife in the village' program. *Population Studies*, 59(1):5-19.

Gertler, P., (2004). Do Conditional Cash Transfers Improve Child Health? Evidence from PROGRESSA's Control Randomized Experiment. *American Economic Review*, 94/2: 336-341.

Gertler, P., and J.W. Molyneaux, (1994). How Economic Development and Family Planning Programs Combined to Reduce Indonesian Fertility. *Demography*, 31/1, 33-63.

Ghuman, Sharon, Behrman, Jere, and Gultiano, Socorro, (2006). Children's Nutrition, School Quality and Primary School Enrollment in the Philippines. *ICSEAD Working Paper Series* Vol. 2006-24.

Glewwe, Paul (2007). The impact of child health and nutrition on education in developing countries: Theory, econometric issues and recent empirical evidence. *Food and Nutrition Bulletion*, 26(2): S235-S250.

Glewwe, Paul and King, Elizabeth (2001). The impact of early childhood nutritional status on cognitive development: Does the timing of malnutrition matter? *The World Bank Economic Review*, 15(1):81-113.

Glewwe, Paul and Miguel, Edward (2007). The impact of child health and nutrition on education in less developed countries. In T. Paul Schultz and John Strauss, eds., *Handbook of Development Economics, Volume 4*, Amsterdam: North Holland Press.

Glewwe, Paul, Jacoby, Hanan and King, Elizabeth. (2001) Early childhood nutrition and academic achievement: a longitudinal analysis. *Journal of Public Economics*, 81(3):345-368.

Glewwe, Paul, Jacoby, Hanan (1995). An economics analysis of delayed primary school enrollment in low income country: The role of early childhood nutrition. *The Review of Economics and Statistics*, 77(1):156-169.

Jayne, T., Strauss, J., Yamano, T. and Molla, D. (2002). Targeting of Food Aid in Rural Ethiopia: Chronic Need or Inertia? *Journal of Development Economics*, 68:247-88.

King, Elizabeth and Behrman, Jere (2009). Timing and Duration of Exposure in Evaluations of Social Programs. *World Bank Research Observer*, 24(1):55-82

Kirono, D.G.C. (2000). *Indonesian seasonal rainfall variability, links to El Nino Southern Oscillation and Agricultural Impacts*, Unpublished PhD Dissertation. Monash University, Australia.

Kirono, D.G.C., Tapper, N.J. and McBride, J.L. (1999). Documenting Indonesian rainfall in the 1997-1998 El Nino event. *Physical Geography*, 20: 422-435.

Maluccio, J.A., J. Hoddinott, J.R. Behrman, R. Martorell, A. R. Quisumbing, and A.D. Stein (2006). The Impact of an Experimental Nutritional Intervention in Childhood on Education among Guatemalan Adults. *FCND Discussion Papers No 207*, IFPRI, Washington DC.

Maluccio, John, Hoddinott, John, Behrman, Jere R., Quisumbing, Agnes, Martorell, Reynaldo and Stein, Aryeh D. (2006). *The impact of nutrition during early childhood on education among Guatemalan adults.* IFPRI, Washington, D.C., Mimeo.

Martorell, R. (1999). The Nature of Child Malnutrition and Its Long-Term Implications. *Food and Nutrition Bulletin* 20: 288–292.

Martorell, Reynaldo (1993). Enhancing Human Potential in Guatemalan Adults Through Improved Nutrition in Early Childhood, *Nutrition Today:* 6-13.

Pitt, M., Rosenzweig, M. and Gibbons, D. (1993). The determinants and consequences of the placement of government programs in Indonesia. *The World Bank Economic Review*, 7:319-348.

Pollitt, Ernesto, (1990). *Malnutrition and Infection in the Classroom.* Paris: UNESCO.

Pollitt, Ernesto, Gorman, Kathleen, Engel, Patrice, Martorell, Reynaldo and Reynaldo Rivera, Reynaldo. (1993) *Early supplementary feeding and cognition*, Monographs of the Society for Research in Child Development, Serial No. 235, Vol. 58, No. 7.

Ravallion, M., (2007). Evaluating Anti-Poverty Program. In T.Paul Schultz and John Strauss, eds, *Handbook of Development Economics, Volume 4*, Amsterdam: North Holland Press.

Rosenzweig, M. and K. Wolpin, (1986). Evaluating the Effects of Optimally Distributed Public Programs. *American Economic Review*, 76:470-482.

Sandjaja, Sihadi, S. Mulyati, Arnelia, M. Saidin, Herudarini, Suhartato, Y. Widodo, A. Atmawikarta, Sudjasmin, Sudikno, I. Zuraedah, (2001). *Studi Dampak Program Makanan Tambahan terhadap Status Gizi dan Kesehatan Bayi dan Anak.* Unpublished Report, PPPG & Bappenas.

Strauss, John, Beegle, Kathleen, Dwiyanto, Agus, Herawati, Yulia, Sikoki, Bondan, and Witoelar, Firman (2004). *The Third Wave of the Indonesia Family Life Survey: Overview and Field Report.* RAND Corp., Santa Monica

Strauss, John, Beegle, Kathleen, Dwiyanto, Agus, Herawati, Yulia, Pattinasarany, Daan, Satriawan, Elan, Sikoki, Bondan, Sukamdi and Witoelar, Firman (2004). *Indonesian Living Standards Before and After the Financial Crisis.* RAND and Institute for Southeast Asian Studies (ISEAS), Santa Monica CA and Singapore.

Strauss, John, and Thomas, Duncan (1995). Human resources: Empirical modeling of household and family decisions. In J.R. Behrman and T.N. Srinivasan, eds, *Handbook of Development Economics, Volume 3A,* Amsterdam: North Holland Press.

Strauss, John, and Thomas, Duncan (1998). Health, nutrition and economic development. *Journal of Economic Literature,* 36(2):766-817.

Strauss, John, and Thomas, Duncan. (2007). Health over the life course. In T.Paul Schultz and John Strauss, eds, *Handbook of Development Economics, Volume 4,* Amsterdam: North Holland Press.

Wooldridge, Jeffrey (2002). *Econometric Analysis of Cross Section and Panel Data.* MIT Press

Wooldridge, Jeffrey (2003). *Introductory Econometrics: A Modern Approach.* Thomson-South Western.

Yamauchi, Chikako (2005). *Evaluating Poverty Alleviation through Microcredit: Methodological and Empirical Evidence from Indonesia.* Department of Economics, UCLA, unpublished paper.

CPSIA information can be obtained at www.ICGtesting.com
Printed in the USA
BVOW07s1713130214

344861BV00008B/149/P